Sidney Crosby

The Story of a Champion

PAUL HOLLINGSWORTH

NIMBUS
PUBLISHING LTD

Nimbus Publishing Limited
PO Box 9166, Halifax, NS
B3K 5M8
(902) 455-4286 nimbus.ca
Printed and bound in Canada

Cover image: The Canadian Press/Claudio Bresciani
Author photo: courtesy CTV Atlantic
Interior design: Jenn Embree

Hollingsworth, Paul, 1969-
    Sidney Crosby : the story of a champion / Paul Hollingsworth.
    ISBN 978-1-55109-791-6
    1. Crosby, Sidney, 1987-. 2. Hockey players—Canada—Biography. 3. Cole Harbour (N.S.)—Biography. I.Arseneault, Paul, 1963- . Sidney Crosby. II. Title.

GV848.5.C76H54 2010   796.962'092   C2010-903076-1

Canada

The Canada Council | Le Conseil des Arts
for the Arts | du Canada

NOVA SCOTIA
Tourism, Culture and Heritage

We acknowledge the financial support of the Government of Canada through the Book Publishing Industry Development Program (BPIDP) and the Canada Council, and of the Province of Nova Scotia through the Department of Tourism, Culture and Heritage for our publishing activities.

SIDNEY CROSBY The Story of a Champion

contents

Acknowledgements

I've been told on many occasions that I have a propensity for hyperbole. I don't possess many natural talents, but I've always conceded that my one true gift is the ability to engage in overstatement. However, in this instance, there are no words available that could possibly describe the gratitude I feel toward several individuals.

With that as a preface, I would like to thank Nimbus Publishing, especially Patrick Murphy, for calling on me to tackle this project. It's a challenge that I've thoroughly enjoyed and I greatly appreciate this opportunity to take my professional career to a new and exciting level. In his thirteen virtues, Benjamin Franklin taught us to "Lose no time and be always employed in something useful." I thought of that magical prose often as I wrote this biography.

My job as reporter/anchor at CTV allows me to work in the very neighbourhood where I grew up and report on stories that matter to me—stories about Nova Scotians and Maritimers. These are "my people" and the job I have is one I cherish. To Mike Elgie, Jay Witherbee, Angela Baxter, Steve Murphy, Peter Mallette, and Leo Carter, I say "thank you" for the opportunity that I continue to cherish. You are all difference-makers in my life, and the gratitude I feel is difficult to express in just a few written lines.

Finally, and most importantly, a few words about my family. The angels smiled on me the day my son, Dawson, was born in 2002 and again in 2006 when my daughter, Jamieson, came into the world. These two perfect souls are the finest young people I know, and my parental pride wells up every time I see their faces. Along with their mother, my wife, Tamara, they make up a golden triangle in my universe—and to borrow once again from Mr. Franklin, they provide the constant felicity of my life.

Introduction

Former UCLA basketball coach John Wooden once said, "The worst thing about new books is that they keep us from reading the old ones." Truer words have never been spoken.

The shelves of libraries and bookstores from coast to coast are crammed with volumes upon volumes of literary classics, novels, biographies, and plays. Perhaps surprisingly, there are now already several Sidney Crosby biographies for readers to choose from. I now offer this "new book," as coach Wooden would call it, for humble submission onto the checklists of North American readers. This book covers the life (albeit, mostly the hockey life) of an extraordinary young Nova Scotia native, Sidney Crosby. (In fact, if I had a second choice for the title of this book, I would have chosen *The Extraordinary Life of Sidney Crosby*. He's that compelling a person.)

It's appropriate that the opening quote is by John Wooden. A titan in the sports world who coached his teams to ten NCAA championships, Wooden, like Crosby, was equipped with more than just God-given talent. He was special. He changed the way fans, players, and journalists viewed the game of basketball. Similarly, by the time Crosby was seventeen years old, he too had altered how we appreciated, and to some extent interpreted, hockey excellence. I'm sure the two never met (Wooden passed away in the spring of 2010), but if they had, the old coach, I'm certain, would have seen in Crosby a personification of the ingredients that make up his tiered approach to winning (in life and in sports). Wooden's Pyramid of Excellence cites industriousness, enthusiasm, skill, confidence, and competitive greatness, to name a few, as being essential traits needed to reach a level of excellence in one's chosen vocation.

I don't pretend to be Crosby's great friend or close confidante. We know each other a little bit and have always gotten along rather well, but the basis of our relationship has always been professional, not personal. However, I have sensed that because I'm from his home province and because we have some friends and cultural experiences in common, he has at times offered me a little more texture in his interviews and a tad more access—especially when I'm on the road working for TSN.

I can cite several examples of such treatment:

When Crosby led the Rimouski Océanic to a Quebec Major Junior Hockey League championship over the Halifax Mooseheads in 2005, he delayed his on-ice celebrations at the Metro Centre with his teammates to give me the time I needed to tape a six-minute interview for TSN's *That's Hockey* (the picture of a patient Crosby answering my questions during this interview is on the back cover of this book). As we spoke, he occasionally glanced over longingly to see the President's Cup being hoisted by teammates, and while his impatience with my questioning would have been understandable, he stayed with me and helped me do my job before he began celebrating the more significant task he had just completed.

If I had to do it over again I would have cut the interview short and let him join in the fun, but the point is even at that young age Crosby seemed to have a keen understanding of what his role was in the hockey world and the complex nature of the responsibilities he was already burdened with. My sense was he knew star hockey players like himself probably should set aside some time—even when inconvenient—for networks like TSN. It was gracious and impressive and a glimpse into the future of how this young man operates in his public dealings.

Another memorable encounter with Crosby came in the minutes before his NHL debut. On October 5, 2005, he played his first regular season game in the National Hockey League on the road against the New Jersey Devils. At that time the Devils still played at Continental Airlines Arena; they have since left for a new facility in nearby Newark. Good thing, because the old rink was not suited for hockey's highest professional league. As a case in point, before

Sidney Crosby gives a television interview between periods of a Rimouski Océanic game.

the game started, I found a small room in which to prepare for my live appearance on TSN's *SportsCentre*. The room I chose appeared to be an abandoned referees' room, so I grabbed a seat, turned on my laptop, and got to work writing my material. However, within minutes I found out that this barren concrete shell, which was best suited to a minor hockey team, was actually the visiting team's (in this case the Pittsburgh Penguins') dressing room. And like a scene from a movie, the first person through the door, carrying his bag, was none other than eighteen-year-old Sidney Crosby. As I packed up my things and prepared to exit, I asked him if he was nervous. He paused from taping his stick, cocked his head, and said, "No, why would I be nervous. Are you nervous?" Smart answer to a stupid question.

Of course he wasn't nervous. When his team lost that game he still found ways to showcase his skill and poise. He tallied his first assist, he certainly didn't look at all nervous during the game or afterward while speaking during countless post-game interviews. He behaved, in a word, wonderfully. He was then, as he is now, and as he was when I first met him in 2001, special.

A special person does special things. He finds the right words to say at just the right time in interviews. He scores seven goals in a game competing against older players. He also scores a hundred points in his rookie NHL season as a teenager, becomes the youngest captain in NHL history to hoist the Stanley Cup, gets named to Canada's Olympic team and then scores the winning goal in overtime of the gold medal game—

Sidney Crosby gives a television interview between periods of a Rimouski Océanic game.

uniting the country the same way Paul Henderson did in 1972. And, my personal favourite: a special person asks you about the weather back in Nova Scotia minutes before a first-ever showdown against the Washington Capitals' Alexander Ovechkin.

These athletic abilities and character traits, I believe, are the secret to knowing and comprehending Sidney Crosby. He has the perfect mix of talent, drive, poise, and grace. One can thank God for most of those qualities, thank his parents for the rest, and thank Sidney Crosby himself if one ever has the opportunity to do so.

TSN's Pierre McGuire once told me that "elite players elevate their game at the most important time." I agree with Pierre's observation, but with Sidney Crosby I'll add the following: Yes he elevates his play at important times, but to him I believe every time is an important time—and not just in hockey. In life, too, he represents an awesome blend of goodness. He's been called a priceless gem. And why not? He's the embodiment of John Wooden's most important layer of his Pyramid of Success—competitive greatness.

The book in your hands explores Sidney Crosby's hockey life to the end of the 2009–2010 season. His life story is not yet complete; his story is still unfolding before our eyes.

But I can guarantee this. Once you read this book you will come to the same incontrovertible conclusion I have reached: Sidney Crosby is special. Special in life and special in hockey.

I also think Coach Wooden would have really liked this guy.

chapter 1

The Early Years

I n Cole Harbour, Nova Scotia, there are two massive road signs. One reads, "Welcome to Cole Harbour." The other: "Home of Sidney Crosby."

Understanding the love between Crosby and his home community may be the central requirement needed when assessing his life story. He loves that he comes from Cole Harbour—and the people there love him for that. He could have chosen to live in Pittsburgh year round but chose not to. His "circle" is small, and to this day the friends and family who matter to him the most live in the neighbourhoods and cul-de-sacs of Cole Harbour. It's where he began his life and where he found early fame. A Cole Harbour Red Wings banner with number 87 on it hangs proudly over the two ice surfaces at Cole Harbour Place, not just because of what he has accomplished in the National Hockey League, but also for his minor hockey exploits that helped him achieve a certain level of national stardom long before he even played junior hockey.

Born in Halifax on August 7, 1987, Sidney Crosby is the son of Trina and Troy. Trina's brothers, Robbie and Harry Forbes, were standout hockey players with the

Halifax Lions of the Metro Valley Junior A Hockey League in the 1980s, while Troy was a goaltender with Verdun of the Quebec Major Junior Hockey League and was drafted in the twelfth round of the 1984 NHL Entry Draft.

Sidney Crosby was not a late bloomer. All evidence points to the fact that he was a gifted, highly coordinated athlete even before he began elementary school. His mother, Trina, told *Sports Illustrated* that her son had never known one day of physical clumsiness in his life. "When [Sidney] threw a baseball it was like he was a twenty-year-old, the form," Trina said. "That sounds ridiculous, I know, but when it came to motor skills, he could do everything."

In addition to his physical abilities, Crosby was also equipped with an un-

common competitive drive at a young age. "He'd call me to hang out when we were kids, and with other guys they're calling to come over and watch movies or play video games," his friend Mike Chiasson told *Sports Illustrated* in the same article. "But with Sid you knew you were always going in his basement to play hockey, have a shootout. His passion, his hard work: That's what got him there."

His hockey-playing days may have started at Cole Harbour Place shortly after he learned to skate at the age of three, but the honing and practicing of those skills has been the ongoing quest of his life. Until he was eight, Troy would play goaltender in the basement of their Cole Harbour home, but as Sidney's shooting ability improved, the

The sign says it all: Cole Harbour loves its favourite son.

young boy soon discovered his father was a less-than-willing combatant. So he would shoot the puck for hours, dent and smudge the family dryer. Always practicing. Always getting better.

If there is one person who holds a unique perspective on Sidney Crosby's hockey bloodlines, it's Darren Cossar, the Executive Director of Hockey Nova Scotia. Cossar remembers seeing Sidney play the game at a young age and recognized the family traits immediately. "I played with his uncle, Robbie Forbes, who was one of the smoothest and skilled players ever to play junior and university hockey in the Maritimes," said Cossar. "And I coached his dad, Troy, in junior. Troy was probably the most competitive and driven player I ever coached. My first comment was Sidney had all the skill and hockey sense of his Uncle Robbie and all the determination, drive, and competitiveness of his dad—a mix that was special to see even in an eleven-year-old. I knew instantly that Sidney was special and Nova Scotia would be represented in a big way at the NHL level."

Sidney was introduced to the game at a young age, and Crosby family legend tells of a young boy wrecking the dryer in the basement by shooting pucks at the appliance repeatedly for years. It didn't take long for all to see that he was equipped with a special gift for the game. Home video shows him as the best player on the ice at ages five and six, even though he was sometimes playing against children two and three years his

Minor Hockey Age Groupings

Novice (ages 5–8)
Atom (ages 9–10)
Peewee (ages 11–12)
Bantam (ages 13–14)
Midget (ages 15–17)
Junior (ages 18–20)

senior. "I coached him on his first team," Paul Gallagher told the *Edmonton Sun* in 2008. "As soon as I saw him, I went to the organizers and said 'Are you sure he's only five? I've never seen a five-year-old kid skate like that.'"

In the same column, Paul Mason, who coached Crosby in peewee, talked about Crosby during those early years. "He had vision beyond vision. My assistant coach and I used to look at each other and say 'Did he do that on purpose?'" Mason remembered taking Crosby's team to the famed Quebec City peewee tournament. "I was trying to tell them there that [Sidney] is pretty special, but when they were promoting the top kids in the tournament, he wasn't one of them. I went and watched some of them and I could tell in seconds that those kids couldn't hold a candle to Sidney. He scored six goals in our first game at the Quebec tournament."

Sidney Crosby as a member of the Dartmouth Subways at the 2002 Air Canada Cup in Bathurst, New Brunswick.

and 'Wait until you see him.' There was nothing special about his size, [he was] maybe a little small if anything, but he was like an adult playing with kids. Sidney had all the control, vision, and concepts of hockey. He still had more to learn, but he understood the game and the puck seemed to follow him or always be around him. In actual fact he was reading the other players, reacting and arriving to where the puck was before anyone else. It was as if he knew where the play was going and what the other kids were thinking."

Describing how good a hockey player Sidney Crosby was as a boy is not an easy task. It's like explaining the beauty of a sunset or why the four movements of Beethoven's Symphony No. 5 represent the best musical composition in history.

In Crosby's case the numbers help. As a fourteen-year-old he totalled almost 200 points playing for the Dartmouth Major Midget AAA Subways. At the 2002 Air Canada Cup he added 24 more points in 7 games. As a fifteen-year-old with Shattuck-St. Mary's, playing against much older players, he set a new record with 162 points in only 57 games and then added 10 goals in 6 games at the USA 17-Under High School Championship, finishing the tournament with 18 points—performances that brought Quebec Major Junior Hockey League scout Denys Faucher to say in 2004: "He does everything on ice. On skates, he is like a Formula One race car, he is so explosive. He passes like a professional, is generous

Darren Cossar tells the story of going to watch Crosby play for the first time—a peewee game in Cole Harbour. "Sidney, Sidney, Sidney, it was all you heard," said Cossar. "From listening to people, it was as if he was the only child playing hockey in Nova Scotia in the late nineties. I doubted he could really be that good and decided I should check this kid out. At the door of the arena I was greeted with, 'Is this your first time?'

with the puck and works very hard." So successful had Crosby become that as a fourteen-year-old he suited up to play for the Dartmouth AAA Major Midget Subways. "He actually made our team as a thirteen-year-old, but Hockey Nova Scotia wouldn't let him play," said Subways head coach Brad Crossley. But Crosby's success did not come without a price. Stories of opposing players attempting to injure him and hockey parents screaming abuse directed his way have rattled around Nova Scotia hockey rinks for years.

Hockey in Canada is serious business—competitive to the hilt. Go to any arena from coast to coast on a Saturday and you'll find a loud and embarrassing hockey parent—or at least you'll find someone who can tell you a horror story about a mom or dad who took their hockey passion a step or two beyond the limits of decorum. Sidney Crosby lived through those horror stories as a child. He faced unimaginable adversity before he was even twelve years old. In February of 2010, in an article called "Destiny's Child," *Sports Illustrated* senior reporter S. L. Price wrote the following:

… as he tore through the Cole Harbour Timbits and Atom and Pee-Wee seasons, his name grew, and with fame came the ugly side of hockey fever. Titles were won, tournaments dominated but resentment festered: He was too good. Whoever stopped him could make a name. By the time Sidney was eleven, he'd sit in the stands during tournaments while waiting for his team's turn to play, wearing shoulder pads but no sweater; too often parents, seeing the name on his jersey, had jeered him to the point of tears…his parents grew frightened. Men in the stands, frustrated at the way Crosby over-

Captain Crosby: Sidney Crosby follows the puck for Nova Scotia at the 2003 Canada Winter Games in Bathurst-Campbellton, New Brunswick.

Sidney Crosby awaits the drop of the puck at the 2002 Air Canada Cup.

shadowed their sons, would yell about breaking his neck, how he was going to get killed; come game time, Sidney found himself slashed, punched, hammered from behind.

Crosby told Price, years later, that the memories of those abuses still lingered. "I remember being in pee-wee, a guy trying to break my leg," Sidney said. "It wasn't even during a play: I was going to a faceoff, and a guy just two-handed it right at my knee—like a baseball bat."

Undaunted, Crosby soldiered on and experienced breathtaking success at a very young age. In his one season with the Subways, he led the team to a second-place finish at the Air Canada Cup National Midget Championship while totalling 217 points in 81 regular season and playoff games. At the Air Canada Cup, playing against the top midget players in the country (who were in some cases two and three years his senior), Crosby was named the tournament's most valuable player, finishing with 18 points in 5 games.

Looking back on the season he coached Crosby, Crossley said Sidney's talent was evident the moment he stepped on the ice at the Dartmouth Sportsplex for the first time. But what also separated him from his peers was his approach. Even at fourteen, Crosby had a professional approach. "He was first at practice and last to leave," said Crossley. "He worked on things on his own in the hallway before practices began and before he went on the ice."

Needing a new challenge and facing increasing attention at home, his parents decided the best course was to get him away from the scrutiny of minor hockey in Nova Scotia. So they chose Shattuck-St. Mary's school in Faribault, Minnesota. For the first time since he was a toddler, Crosby could play hockey and avoid the type of media attention he was getting back in Nova Scotia. And despite the pain of seeing their son move away from home at age fifteen, the Crosbys could rest assured knowing he was no longer performing in potentially toxic environments like he'd been growing accustomed to back home. But his absence from home took its toll on his family, as Price wrote in *Sports Illustrated*: "His one year there—he won a seventeen-and-under national championship—left Trina and his little sister, Taylor, heartbroken. But Troy was all but in mourning. For the first time, he couldn't be in the stands to see Sidney."

"It was my first experience away from Nova Scotia, and I had to catch up academically," Crosby said in an interview with *ESPN The Magazine*. "I struggled with it at first. But I loved the atmosphere. You can have friendships wherever you play, but at Shattuck, you lived

Sidney Crosby celebrates a goal as a member of the Dartmouth Subways at the 2002 Air Canada Cup.

Crosby as a member of the Shattuck-St. Mary's hockey team.

together, went to class together, travelled and played together. You get to know each other, everyone, a lot faster and a lot better." Faster and better led to several long-lasting friendships. Future NHL players Drew Stafford and Jack Johnson were teammates and classmates of Crosby's. While they would all go their separate ways en route to the NHL, the trio has remained close over the years. In fact, Crosby has been known to host his former Sabres teammates in Nova Scotia during the summer months.

Crosby played just one year at Shattuck-St. Mary's, but it was a memorable one. In just 57 games he scored 72 goals and 90 assists while leading the Sabres to a United States national midget championship. Beyond his on-ice success, Crosby seemed to thrive in the relative anonymity of playing for his new team, away from the growing spotlight that had been enveloping him the previous year with the Subways. "I think he liked the fact that he didn't get special treatment," his coach Tom Ward said. "He had to try out like everyone else. And I think at some level he knew this was going to be the last time he was just Sid from Halifax, not Sidney Crosby, hockey star."

Shattuck-St. Mary's

Shattuck-St. Mary's is a school with a rich hockey history. The school boasts a who's who of hockey players and coaches. Zach Parise played there for four years, and for a while his father—former NHL player J. P., who played for Canada in the 1972 Summit Series against the USSR—was his coach. Other notable players to skate for the Sabres at Shattuck-St. Mary's include Jack Johnson, Jonathan Toews, and Drew Stafford.

During two weeks late in the winter of 2003, Crosby returned to the Maritimes to play hockey for Nova Scotia at the Canada Winter Games in Bathurst and Campbellton, New Brunswick. After returning to Faribault to close out the school year, it became apparent that Crosby—like the previous year with the Dartmouth Subways—had outgrown his surroundings. He needed a new challenge to help continue his hockey development.

Sidney Crosby winds up for a shot in a game with Shattuck-St. Mary's.

In His Own Words

The first time I interviewed Sidney Crosby I couldn't get over his cool composure, confidence, and intelligence. He had yet to play his first NHL game, but he was already commenting with insight on the ways the settlement that ended the players' lockout would change the game. His birth certificate said teenager, his conduct revealed an older soul. I've interviewed political leaders who were older but not wiser.

Sidney wore shorts to that first interview and his thick thighs barely fit in the chair. They were at least as broad as the shoulders on which the future of the game was about to rest. At the end of the interview, Sid was mobbed by staff members looking for autographs for their kids, myself included. After signing them all, he spoke about taking public transit to the gym at Saint Mary's University and so far as I know that's exactly what he did. One can only imagine the bus driver's reaction when the future superstar dropped in his $1.50.

STEVE MURPHY
CTV Atlantic news anchor

chapter 2

Far from Home

S idney Crosby would later say leaving Shattuck-St. Mary's was one of the most difficult decisions of his life. But his one year with Shattuck-St. Mary's helped make him the number one selection in the Quebec Major Junior Hockey League draft in 2003. While his exploits at Shattuck-St. Mary's did not exactly make headline news north of the border, junior hockey scouts, coaches, and executives had paid close attention to his performance. When Crosby finished playing for the Dartmouth Subways, he was considered a local Maritime hockey phenom worthy of national attention. One year later he was universally dubbed a can't-miss prospect—and the most coveted player heading into the QMJHL draft. He was widely considered a lock to reach the NHL as an impact player within a couple of seasons. Living up to the billing, Crosby's first preseason game for Rimouski saw him score eight points—a portent of what was to come.

Prior to Crosby joining the team, the Rimouski Océanic had led a rags-to-riches-to-rags existence in the QMJHL. Founded in 1995, the Océanic, buoyed by sellout

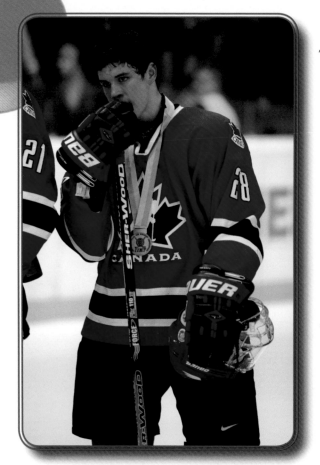

they chose Crosby. That selection soon turned the franchise's fortunes around. The Océanic built a solid support cast around Crosby, and the team was once again championship-calibre, playing before sellout crowds. The Océanic now received media attention from TV networks, newspapers, and magazines from across North America.

In 2003–2004, his first season with Rimouski, Crosby was named Canadian Hockey League Rookie of the Year and Player of the Year after leading the league (which consists of the Quebec Major Junior and Ontario and Western Hockey Leagues) in scoring with 54 goals and 81 assists. He followed that up with 16 points in 9 playoff games for the Océanic.

Even more impressive was that Crosby was the scoring leader despite having missed several weeks of the QMJHL schedule in December to play for Canada at the World Junior Hockey Championship in Helsinki. There, he set a new record, becoming the youngest player—at sixteen years, four months, and twenty-one days—in the history of the tournament to score a goal, when he scored against Switzerland in a 7–2 victory. Canada settled for a silver medal, and Crosby finished the tournament with two goals and three assists in six games. By no means were Crosby's five points a dominating performance, but he was younger than most of his teammates, so the fact that he managed to hold his own proved that he would be a special player.

crowds and young superstars like Brad Richards and Vincent Lecavalier, were a model of success during their first five seasons, culminating with a Memorial Cup championship in 2000. But the team soon fell into rebuilding mode, and smaller crowds were the norm at Colisée de Rimouski amid poorer regular season records. In 2002–03, the Océanic finished with just 25 points in 72 games, by far the worst record in the league—but in finishing last they had earned the right to select first in the draft, and

Crosby's 2004 teammates included future NHL players Jeff Carter and Dion Phaneuf and future Pittsburgh Penguin teammate Marc-André Fleury, but he also competed in the tournament with some company from his home province. Stephen Dixon, a Halifax native and member of the Cape Breton Screaming Eagles of the QMJHL, also made the Canadian roster. It was the first time in tournament history that two Nova Scotia natives had made Canada's roster.

For his two seasons in the QM-JHL, Crosby was a veritable travelling road show. Everywhere he played, the crowds were huge. Ten thousand at the Halifax Metro Centre, eleven thousand at le Colisée in Quebec City, seven thousand at the Moncton Coliseum—people wanted to see him play in person. They didn't always cheer, in fact they often booed (even in Halifax), but the more he played, the more he shone, and the clearer it became that he would be soon NHL-ready.

As his comfort zone increased, so too did his ability to adapt to the culture of northern Quebec. Within months of joining the Océanic, Crosby was conducting interviews fluently in French, an effort that resonated with the Quebec populace. Over the decades the province, the language, and the culture had taken a beating from English Canada. But here was a handsome young English-Canadian, a can't-miss superstar, who not only enjoyed playing in Quebec—he embraced it.

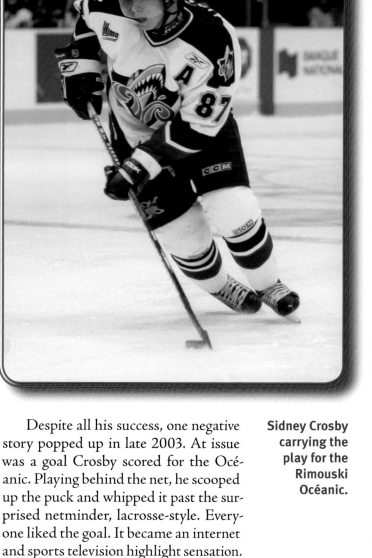

Despite all his success, one negative story popped up in late 2003. At issue was a goal Crosby scored for the Océanic. Playing behind the net, he scooped up the puck and whipped it past the surprised netminder, lacrosse-style. Everyone liked the goal. It became an internet and sports television highlight sensation. Don Cherry didn't like the goal one bit, and he said so on his "Coach's Corner" segment on *Hockey Night in Canada*. "I like the kid, but I've seen him now after

Sidney Crosby carrying the play for the Rimouski Océanic.

Crosby's emergence as a QMJHL star meant tickets to Océanic games were scarce.

rantings about Crosby seemed to lose steam. Perhaps it was because not many people agreed with him. The *Globe and Mail*'s William Houston responded to a slight directed at Crosby by writing that Cherry was "a disservice to the telecast and the viewers."

Maybe Cherry listened to his detractors. Perhaps he tired of the subject—or to be fair, perhaps Crosby legitimately changed his on-ice habits to the point of rehabilitation in the eyes of Don Cherry. Whatever happened, over time, Cherry seemed to let up on his criticisms of Crosby (even to the point of complimenting the Pittsburgh captain on his play and leadership in the 2009 playoffs).

With each passing season, Crosby had developed a trend that saw his play improve on a year-by-year basis. His one season at Shattuck-St. Mary's was a level above his play the year before with the Dartmouth Subways. With that pattern in mind, if his rookie season in the QMJHL was dominating, Crosby's sophomore campaign was staggering. Another CHL scoring title: 66 goals and 102 assists. A second consecutive CHL Player of the Year Award. Another roster spot on Canada's World Junior team in Grand Forks, North Dakota. Crosby would score nine points in six games, helping Canada win a gold medal. Halifax's Stephen Dixon was once again on the Team Canada roster and by capturing the gold medal, Crosby and Dixon became the first two Nova Scotia natives to win a World Junior Hockey Championship since Sydney's Paul Boutilier.

some goals, and he's doing stuff, he's sliding on his stomach…he's hotdogging," said Cherry.

When Don Cherry speaks, the hockey world listens. Whether he's wrong, right, bigoted, empathetic, or starkly ill-informed, hockey people always seem to listen to what he has to say—and they definitely listened this time, as his reaction became headline news across the country. Perhaps sensing that he had caused a stir, Cherry piled it on for the next several years. He ripped Crosby for skipping a prospects game and repeatedly chastised the teenager for embellishing injuries on the ice and sneeringly called him a "whiner" and a "golden boy." As time passed, Cherry's

On August 8, 2009, the day after his twenty-second birthday and the day following his Stanley Cup parade in Cole Harbour, Crosby paid a visit to the Nova Scotia Sport Hall of Fame in Halifax. Crosby has not yet been inducted into the hall, although he will be someday. In the meantime, Executive Director Bill Robinson has ensured the shrine pays special homage to Crosby's accomplishments by displaying many of his hockey artifacts and memorabilia.

Encased in glass are old gloves, skates, sticks, programs, photographs, and newspaper articles. But off to the side, for all to not only see but also touch, is the dryer. The very dryer that Crosby damaged beyond usefulness during those years of practice in his Cole Harbour basement.

On this day, as a way to round out his homecoming celebration, Crosby brought some friends and family members along for a private viewing. "He was really taken back by it," said Robinson. "The first thing he saw and the first thing he went to was the dryer. At one point he actually put the Stanley Cup on the dryer. He was smiling the entire time. It was a special moment."

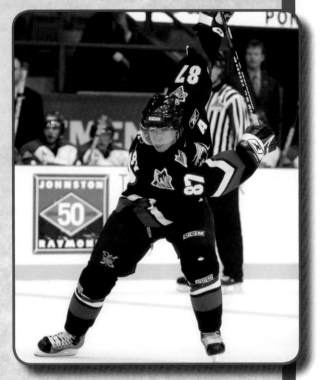

Sidney Crosby takes a shot in a game against the Moncton Wildcats.

Robinson says the Crosby display remains one of the more popular attractions at the Nova Scotia Sport Hall of Fame, and with contributions from the Crosby family, the display will continue to expand to help celebrate the accomplishments of the best hockey player in Nova Scotia history.

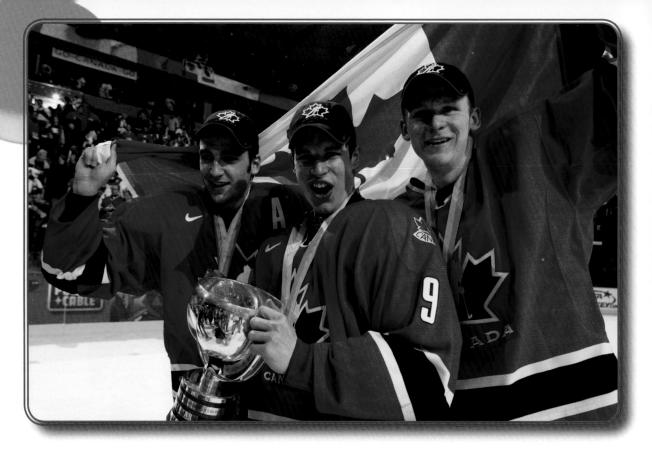

Sidney Crosby celebrates Canada's gold medal at the 2005 World Junior Hockey Championship with Patrice Bergeron (left) and Corey Perry (right).

Following the QMJHL regular season Crosby added 31 points in just 13 playoff games to lead Rimouski to its second Presidents Cup in franchise history with a four-game series sweep over the Halifax Mooseheads in the championship final. Crosby was also named playoff MVP. For the teenager who had left home at a young age, his championship moment fittingly came on home ice as the Océanic won the series clincher before more than ten thousand fans at the Halifax Metro Centre, with Crosby's family and friends in attendance. The victory over Halifax put Rimouski back in the Memorial Cup for the first time since the Brad Richards–led Océanic won the 2000 Memorial Cup in Halifax.

For several reasons, media attention at the 2005 Memorial Cup was extremely high. With NHL players in the midst of a season-stopping lockout, the tournament served as a void filler for North American hockey fans who had suffered through a long winter without being able to watch the game's best players. The Memorial Cup also featured two terrific junior hockey teams. Rimouski, led by Crosby, had attracted consistent media attention throughout the 2004–05 season. The host London Knights,

though not as famous as the Océanic, were coached by former Quebec Nordique and Washington Capital centre Dale Hunter, and were led on the ice by right wing Corey Perry, who topped the Knights in scoring with 113 points and had been a teammate of Crosby's at the World Junior Hockey Championship five months earlier.

With ten thousand fans packing the Labatt Centre on a nightly basis, it became apparent that London and Rimouski were the top two teams in the week-long tournament. Crosby led the tournament in scoring with eleven points and his team's only round-robin

loss was a 4–3 overtime decision to London in the opening game. The teams played a rematch in the final on May 29, 2005. The Knights won the game 4–0 and captured the first Memorial Cup in team history.

The loss brought the curtain down on Crosby's brief two-year major junior hockey career. Not yet eighteen years old, Crosby had little left to accomplish with the Océanic. In 2002 he left the Dartmouth Subways for Shattuck-St. Mary's. In 2003 he bolted for the Quebec Major Junior Hockey League. Now he was ready for the National Hockey League—or at least, so said the experts.

Sidney Crosby waits for the puck in a game against the Czech Republic at the 2005 World Junior Hockey Championship.

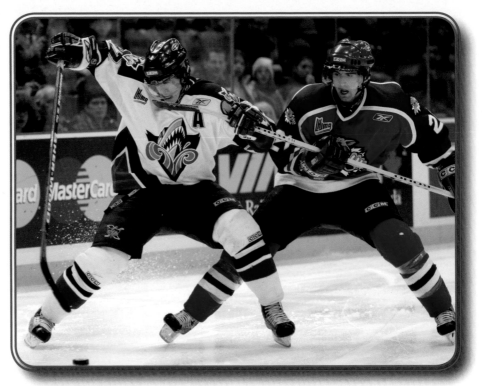

Sidney Crosby fights off the check of a Moncton Wildcats defender.

(Opposite page) Sidney Crosby as a rookie with the Océanic.

"He's outgrown the league and I don't mean any disrespect to the Canadian Hockey League," TSN's Pierre McGuire said following the Memorial Cup. "Sidney Crosby is that good."

On July 13, 2005, the NHL and the NHL Players' Association reached a new collective bargaining agreement and ended the work stoppage that had cancelled the 2004–2005 NHL season. But where would Crosby play? Because the previous season had been cancelled, the 2005 draft lottery theoretically left every team in the hunt to pick first overall and the chance to draft Sidney Crosby. The draft order was settled on July 22, with the Pittsburgh Penguins winning the first overall pick. There

was never any doubt, of course, that the Penguins would select Crosby. Within hours of the lottery, Penguins player and owner Mario Lemieux told reporters that Crosby would be the catalyst to rebuild the franchise into a Stanley Cup contender.

Sidney Crosby had burst onto the world hockey stage four years earlier as a dominant midget player for the Dartmouth Subways. Now he was a teammate of Mario Lemieux, with whom he would live during the season. The summer before Crosby entered the NHL included an appearance on the *Tonight Show* with Jay Leno, and his image was omnipresent on Gatorade and Reebok television commercials. Before he even played a game,

Sidney Crosby and then-Penguins general manager Craig Patrick meet with the media in 2005.

Sidney Crosby was now the face and the future of not only the Pittsburgh Penguins, but the "new NHL." The league had just closed its doors for the entire season, and now, as it prepared to mend fences with its fans, the league was putting Crosby at the forefront of how it marketed the NHL brand. Already one of the most famous hockey players in the world, Crosby was also one of the NHL's most important marketing tools.

Looking ahead to the season and the years ahead, Pierre McGuire was prophetic in assessing the skill set Crosby would bring to the NHL. "You will see it when he goes to the NHL, he's going to make the coach a lot smarter. He's going to make the organization look stronger and he's going to make the players around him that much better. He's a winner and a champion and there's brilliant things coming forward for Sidney Crosby."

chapter 3

The Rookie

Sidney Crosby arrived in Pittsburgh armed with such an accomplished hockey resumé that he was considered a franchise cornerstone capable of elevating the Penguins to a level of success not witnessed since the team won back-to-back Stanley Cup titles in the early 1990s.

Only eighteen years of age at the start of his first NHL season, Crosby was already a world-class athlete, possessing the physical gifts and personality traits that set him apart from his peers. While most hockey observers predicted he would be an impact NHL player as a rookie, Crosby said publicly (and modestly) on many occasions that his top priority was just to make the Penguins roster. "I'm looking at it as short-term as possible. I want to have a good camp and push myself to raise my game as best I can," Crosby said. "Obviously, this is a new level, but the pressure has always been there. I've always put a lot of pressure on myself to perform."

With number 87 coming to town, the Penguins went to work improving the rest of their roster. Forward Mark Recchi, who first played for the Penguins from

The rookie and the veteran: Crosby and teammate Mark Recchi in 2005.

1988–92, re-signed with Pittsburgh as a free agent after the 2003–04 season. Soon, he was joined by defencemen Sergei Gonchar and Lyle Odelein, forwards Ziggy Palffy and John LeClair, and goaltender Jocelyn Thibault. "Playing with those guys is great, but practicing is where you are really going to benefit, just by seeing their habits," said Crosby. "It's going to help me. As for the team, to have that many guys come in, to sign that many guys is just a great situation for everyone." These new players, including Crosby, the young centrepiece, were part of a plan to make the team competitive again and help it reconnect with its dwindling fan base. (In 2003–04, the team averaged 11,877 fans a game, lowest in the league.)

Following a short summer off-season, Crosby moved in with Penguins owner and captain Mario Lemieux, who had suggested the arrangement after the entry draft. After only a few days at his new home, Crosby knew his living situation was going to be a great learning experience. "I've been talking to him a lot to learn little things," said Crosby. "He's got a great family. It's a good environment for me to be in. I'm just trying to learn as much as I can."

If there was one player in the league that Crosby could learn from, it was Lemieux. Like Crosby, Lemieux came to the NHL after dominating the QMJHL. In two hundred regular season games with the Laval Voisins from 1981–84, Lemieux had scored 562 points. He knew the pressures, the media requirements, and understood that Crosby would benefit from a more sheltered off-ice environment while dealing with the scrutiny. "I got some attention but not like he's getting," said Lemieux, as he reflected on his own rookie season more than two decades ago. "Especially in Canada and especially here in Pittsburgh."

Training camp for the Pittsburgh Penguins 2005–06 season began on September 16, 2005. A small market team that had finished last in the thirty-team NHL before the lockout, the Penguins were suddenly the media's main focus, and Crosby's first training camp was truly an unprecedented spectacle. All four Canadian sports channels—TSN, The Score, RDS, and Sportsnet—had crews on location for extensive coverage. In some cases, reporters filed more than one story a day and broadcasted live for network supper-hour shows appearing north of the border. Four major Canadian newspapers—the *Montreal Gazette*, *Toronto Star* and *Sun*, and the *Globe and Mail*—sent reporters to Pittsburgh to cover the camp. The *Globe and Mail*, sensing that Crosby would not be a fleeting storyline, even assigned reporter Shawna Richer to the team for the entire regular season so she could document his every shift. Richer accumulated such a treasure trove of Crosby information that she later wove the entire season into a bestselling biography, *The Rookie: A Season with Sidney Crosby and the New NHL*.

Taking all the attention in stride, Crosby fit in quickly with his new team. On October 8, 2005—three days after their debut against the Devils—the Penguins kicked off their home schedule against the Boston Bruins, and Crosby scored the first goal of his NHL career. Considering his flare for the dramatic, Crosby's first goal was fairly

Sidney Crosby during a NHL photo shoot. Media interest in the rookie was high before he had even played a single game.

To be considered a rookie, a player must not have played in twenty-five or more NHL games in any preceding seasons, or in six or more NHL games in each of any two preceding seasons. The age of the player is also a determining factor. Any player at least twenty-six years of age by September 15 of that season is not considered a rookie.

Alexander Ovechkin entered the NHL as a twenty-year-old rookie blessed with blazing speed and an incredible shot. In his first career game on October 5, 2005, Ovechkin scored twice against Columbus, serving notice that he would have a tremendous impact in the league. But was he a rookie? Ovechkin had played part of four seasons with the Russian Elite League's Moscow Dynamo, a professional league that paid its players, which by NHL rules would negate Ovechkin's rookie status, and leave him ineligible for the Calder Trophy. But the interpretation of what constitutes a professional league is not an exact formula. For example, the quality of play in the QMJHL is better than some of the lower-level European professional leagues. In the end it was determined, but not without controversy, that Ovechkin was an eligible rookie—paving the way for him to capture the 2005–06 Calder Trophy.

underwhelming, the result of a not-so-spectacular goalmouth scramble. With 1:16 to go in a Penguins power play and his team clinging to a 5–4 lead, Mark Recchi dumped a loose puck toward the net. When goaltender Hannu Toivonen's sprawling kick save sent the puck to his left, Crosby was there to score into a wide open net, giving Pittsburgh a two-goal lead and the opening night crowd something to cheer about. Crosby finished the game with a goal and two assists, but the Penguins lost 7–6 in overtime. After the game, Crosby lamented the Penguins' loss more than he celebrated his first-ever goal. "It's something you dream about, scoring in the NHL," Crosby said. "There's a lot of emotion that comes out of that. But it would have been nice if we had finished it off."

While Crosby's career was off to a solid start, the Penguins soon discovered they were not as strong as team

captain Mario Lemieux predicted during the preseason. The Penguins did not win their first game of the season until October 27, a 7–5 topping of the Atlanta Thrashers. The start would prove to be portentous, as the Penguins were on their way to having the second-worst record in the NHL. Despite their struggles, the Penguins and Crosby did enjoy a few bright spots. The first one came on November 10 in Crosby's first game against the Montreal Canadiens, the team he cheered for growing up in Cole Harbour.

Pittsburgh opened the scoring on a Crosby power play goal in the first period and Lemieux made it 2–0 soon after. But the Canadiens rallied. Craig Rivet closed the gap to 2–1 late in the second period, and Christopher Higgins tied it

at two with just 3:31 to go in the third period, forcing overtime. It appeared Montreal would emerge with the come-from-behind victory, out-shooting the Penguins 6–2 in the extra period. But former Canadien Jocelyn Thibault came through with several game-saving stops for the Penguins, and the game headed to a shootout. Michael Ryder, Mark Recchi, Alexei Kovalev, Mario Lemieux, and Alexander Perezhogin all failed to score, leaving the final opportunity of the first round to Sidney Crosby. With his father in the stands, 16,254 fans standing and cheering, and several hundred thousand more watching the game in Canada on TSN, Crosby broke in from centre ice. He kicked his leg, deked Montreal goalie Jose Theodore, and flipped the puck into the

Sidney Crosby and Alexander Ovechkin at the 2007 NHL All-Star Game. The two young talents quickly became the stars of their sport.

Sidney Crosby scores in a shootout against New York Rangers goalie Henrik Lundqvist.

meshing at the top of the net, sending Theodore's water bottle into the air, and winning the game for the Pens.

The goal was a spectacular play, and the team celebrated as if it had just won a championship. After the game, Crosby acknowledged that defeating the team he worshipped as a child was one of the bigger thrills of his young career. "It's so amazing, it's hard to believe," Crosby said. His captain also weighed in, discussing the poise the eighteen-year-old displayed in a pressure-packed moment. "He's quite amazing. It's great to be on the ice with him," Mario Lemieux said. "He just came out with a great play on that shot."

Another big moment filled with even more intense media pressure came two weeks later on home ice against the Washington Capitals, a team featuring fellow rookie Alexander Ovechkin. Two years older than Crosby, Ovechkin had been drafted first overall by the Capitals in 2004—one year before Crosby—and was already a rookie sensation in his own right. The duo's exciting style of play was already drawing comparisons to another high-scoring NHL pair, Wayne Gretzky and Mario Lemieux. Speaking with reporters the day before the game against Washington, Crosby downplayed the Gretzky-Lemieux comparisons. "We've played twenty games or twenty-one games, so to compare us to Mario and Gretzky is a little early," said Crosby. "I think that we have a lot to prove before we can put ourselves at that level."

Although both had helped energize the NHL fan base in the aftermath of the cancelled 2004–05 season, the two players employed widely different styles of play. Crosby was a fleet-footed finesse player who excelled with incredible on-ice vision and playmaking. Ovechkin possessed those attributes, but he played a more physical game and scored more goals than Crosby did. Other comparisons between the two were mostly unfavourable for Crosby. While Ovechkin was receiving a lot of good press for goals and punishing hits, not all of the media attention directed at Crosby was positive. In several games, including a home-and-home series against cross-state rival Philadelphia, Crosby was accused of being a diver (a player who drops to the ice in an attempt to draw a penalty against the opposition).

All of these distractions and media reports were coming together to create a dramatic setting for Crosby and Ovechkin. Dozens of reporters from across North America were on hand to cover the game. "For me I have to approach it like another game," said Crosby following the pre-game skate. "Obviously there's a lot of excitement around it. I'm up for it." The game itself was close, a 5–4 Penguins victory. As for the individual showdown, Crosby narrowly outperformed his rival by scoring a goal and adding an assist, while Ovechkin registered one assist. The game itself was not meaningful, given that both teams were not close to being playoff contenders. But the showdown between these two was a hint at grander competition. Ovechkin and Crosby were two of the NHL's biggest young stars. The next decade would be defined not only by their play for their respective teams, but also by their head-to-head matchups. This was the first one, but there would be many more to come.

Even with Crosby and the other off-season additions, the 2005–06 Pittsburgh Penguins were not a very good hockey team. In fact, they were performing almost as badly as they had prior to the NHL lockout. By mid-December the team had a dismal 8–17–6 record, and general manager Craig Patrick fired head coach Ed Olczyk and replaced him with former Montreal Canadiens head coach Michel Therrien. The first major shift under Therrien was that the new coach named Crosby the Penguins assistant captain. "This is a new beginning for our team. And [Crosby] is one of our best players," Therrien explained. Therrien dismissed the suggestion that the move put more pressure on the young star. "I don't think it's pressure," said Therrien. "He's a young kid, but sometimes a young kid has good, new ideas."

Not everyone agreed with Therrien. (Hockey Night in Canada commentator Don Cherry was quick to find fault, for one.) In the end, the move didn't make much of a difference—the Penguins remained mired in a dismal season. Another blow to the organization came on January 25, 2006, when Mario Lemieux announced his final retirement from the NHL. At age forty, and having suffered through a multitude of injuries—as

The Calder Memorial Trophy is given annually to the player selected as the "most proficient in his first year of competition in the National Hockey League." The winner is selected by a panel from the Professional Hockey Writers' Association at the end of the regular season. Playoff performances by rookies are not taken into account.

From 1936 until he died in 1943, former NHL president Frank Calder bought a trophy each year to be given permanently to the outstanding rookie. After Calder's death, the NHL presented the Calder Memorial Trophy in his memory and the trophy is to be handed out in perpetuity.

well as cancer—throughout his career, the Penguins captain/owner had been diagnosed with an irregular heartbeat. Rather than risk his health any further, Lemieux decided to end his playing career.

Reaction from around the league was unanimous in praising Lemieux for his on-ice accomplishments and overall contribution to hockey. The moment was also filled with symbolism—a passing of the torch from the previous generation to the newer and younger talent that had entered the NHL. Wayne Gretzky acknowledged that factor within hours of Lemieux's announcement. "The good news is we've got some good, young players, like Crosby and Ovechkin, coming along," said Gretzky. "So I'm sure they'll carry the torch."

Sidney Crosby's rookie season was, by any measure, a tremendous success. After being left off Canada's roster at the 2006 Torino Winter Olympics, he enjoyed a two-week break at home in Cole Harbour and then rejoined the Penguins to finish the season on a torrid scoring pace. On April 17, 2006, in the Penguins' second-last regular season game, Crosby recorded three assists to help lift his team to a 6–1 victory over the New York Islanders. The three points lifted Crosby to the 100-point threshold, making him the youngest player in NHL history to reach the mark, and only the second eighteen-year-old (Dale Hawerchuk was the first).

The next night the Penguins finished the regular season in Toronto with a 5–3 loss to the Maple Leafs. Crosby

scored his 39th goal of the season and recorded his 63rd assist to finish his rookie season with 102 points. "One hundred points would be one [of the highlights]," Crosby said of his rookie year. "After the Olympic break it was a lot of fun playing with this group. We weren't winning as much, but I can't see other teams in the same situation reacting the way we did." The two points on the final night of the season also broke Mario Lemieux's team record for points by a rookie, set in 1984–85. "It's an accomplishment, for sure," Crosby said. "Just to be mentioned with him is an honour."

Following the season, Crosby joined the Canadian team at the World Hockey Championship, where the team finished in fourth place. Then it was off to the NHL awards in June. Along with

Sidney Crosby at top speed at the 2006 IIHF World Championship.

Ovechkin and defenceman Dion Phaneuf of the Calgary Flames, Crosby was a finalist for the Calder Trophy. Before the regular season began most hockey pundits assumed that Ovechkin had a slight advantage over Crosby because he was two years older. Ovechkin had also played a few seasons for Moscow Dynamo in the Russian Elite League, an experience that was a significant step up from Crosby's two years with Rimouski. In the end, the award did wind up going to Ovechkin, who recorded 106 points compared to Crosby's 102.

chapter four

Sophomore Superstar

Sidney Crosby began his second NHL season much the same as his first. Even though Mario Lemieux was no longer a teammate, Crosby once again moved in with Lemieux's family after vacationing during the summer months in Cole Harbour.

Behind the scenes the Penguins had made some changes. For starters, long-time general manager Craig Patrick was let go on July 1 when his contract was not renewed after seventeen seasons. Within weeks the organization hired Ray Shero as Patrick's successor. A former assistant general manager with Nashville and Ottawa, the forty-three-year-old Shero was a youthful match for a team coming off a disappointing finish the previous year but still considered a future contender. "Everyone in the hockey world knows about the Penguins' young talent, and the tremendous potential that we have here," said Shero when he accepted the position. "I'm looking forward to working with the players, coaches and staff—and I can't wait to get started."

For years, even with the presence of Mario Lemieux and then Sidney Crosby, the Penguins were constantly in financial trouble. One reason was Mellon Arena, the oldest rink and lowest revenue-generator among NHL buildings. Lemieux had always maintained that in order for the team to survive in Pittsburgh, a new arena had to built. After a deal with a local casino (one that would have included the construction of a new facility) fell through, Lemieux announced the team was officially for sale. In October 2006, billionaire Jim Balsillie, the CEO of Research in Motion, announced his intent to purchase the Penguins for $185 million (U.S.). But Balsillie made no secret of his intention to move the team to Canada, and when NHL commissioner Gary Bettman told him his impending purchase would have relocation restrictions tied to it, Balsillie backed out. This failed purchase set into a motion a process with the state of Pennsylvania that, in the end, secured a new arena for the Penguins and resulted in Lemieux deciding not to sell the team after all. It was an awkward time for the organization and its players, but it settled the Penguins' fate and secured the franchise in Pittsburgh. In October 2010, the Penguins moved into a brand new arena, the Consol Energy Center, thus ensuring the Penguins' long-term viability.

The 2006–07 Penguins had a different look on the ice as well. Joining the team were two impressive rookies—Jordan Staal and Evgeni Malkin. Malkin had been drafted by the Penguins second overall at the 2004 NHL entry draft, but spent three seasons playing for Metallurg Magnitogorsk in the Russian Super League. (In a strange turn of events, Malkin was forced to flee his team on a road trip in order to pursue his dream of playing in the NHL—the result of a dispute over a transfer agreement between Russian teams and the NHL). Even though his long-awaited NHL debut was delayed after a preseason shoulder injury, Malkin's rookie season still saw him total 85 points in 78 games and capture the Calder Trophy as the NHL's top rookie.

Jordan Staal's journey to Pittsburgh was less tumultuous, but he had just as significant an impact. Just eighteen years old heading into training camp, Staal was thought to be a long shot to make the Penguins when Shero surprisingly named the 2006 first round draft pick to the Penguins' regular season roster.

"Jordan has earned his spot on our roster and deserves to play at the National Hockey League level," Shero said. "We all knew about his skill level when we drafted him, but his work ethic, maturity, and consistent effort have enabled him to make what is normally a difficult transition for a teenager." With Crosby, Staal, Malkin, and a solid mix of veteran players, it appeared, at least on paper, that Pittsburgh had the potential to be a vastly improved squad from the previous season.

Unlike the previous season when the Penguins did not compete for a playoff spot, 2006–07 was a much different story, as the Penguins went from underachievers to Stanley Cup contenders. On January 13, the Penguins travelled to Philadelphia with an 18–17–7 record. A 5–3 victory over the Flyers started a stunning streak of sixteen games without losing in regulation time. When the streak ended, Pittsburgh was cruising toward a playoff spot with a 32–17–9 record.

Behind the team's improved play was Sidney Crosby. The NHL's leading scorer at the all-star break with 64 points, nineteen-year-old Crosby became the youngest player selected to an All-Star Game, garnering the most fan votes (825,783). The game was held in Dallas, and Crosby, who played on a line with Ovechkin and Brendan Shanahan, was held pointless as the Eastern Conference lost to the Western Conference 12–9. "You'd think with all the goals scored out there, I'd have been able to

get in on one of them," Crosby joked. Even Wayne Gretzky, to whom Crosby was often compared, was held pointless in his first all-star game, a fact Crosby found encouraging when told after the game. "Maybe I'll sleep a little easier tonight," he remarked.

Crosby had quickly become one of NHL's most popular players—and the transition from junior hockey phenom to the All-Star Game's leading vote-getter was remarkably quick. However, his task of transforming the Penguins back into a Stanley Cup contender would prove to be a more arduous process. Recent history had been unkind to the Penguins franchise. Between 2001 and 2006, the team had lost seventy-nine games more than it had won. With a playoff berth usually out of reach by early spring, the

Michel Therrien rallies his young Penguins, Crosby (left) and Evgeni Malkin (right).

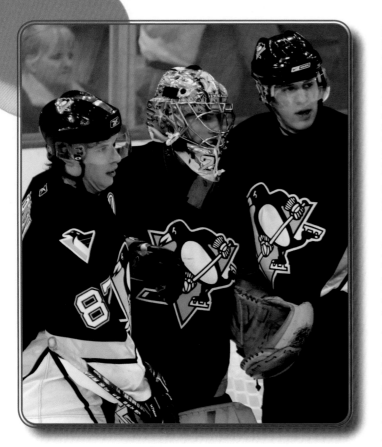

Crosby (left), Marc-André Fleury (centre) and Evgeni Malkin (right) celebrate a Penguins victory. The three first-round draft picks became the core of the young Pittsburgh team.

gary Flames in 1984, three years before Crosby was even born. Roberts was a leader, had won a Stanley Cup with the Flames in 1989, and had performed well for the Toronto Maple Leafs in previous playoff appearances. While Roberts had hoped to be traded to an Ontario-based team, he welcomed the move to Pittsburgh and the opportunity to play for a team loaded with young stars that were becoming the talk of the NHL.

The other player Shero acquired at the trading deadline was Georges Laraque from the Phoenix Coyotes. A renowned fighter, Laraque gave the Penguins more toughness and provided Crosby with more on-ice protection. Throughout Crosby's rookie season and through the first half of the 2006–07 season, hockey analysts had complained that the Penguins were not doing enough to insulate Crosby from the day-to-day physical abuse that takes place in the NHL. With Laraque in the lineup, the thinking went, it was unlikely that other players would continue to take liberties with number 87. The 2006–07 Penguins had youth, speed, skill, size, and veteran flavour sprinkled throughout the lineup. Now they had much-needed toughness. All of these were considered crucial ingredients for a successful playoff run.

Still, the biggest and most important ingredient, by far, was Sidney Crosby. One year after his breakthrough rookie season, Crosby elevated his performance and quickly established himself as the most exciting player in the

team would traditionally audition players from the minor leagues and perhaps trade away a high-salaried player for prospects or future draft picks. But this year would be different. The team was playing well. Sidney Crosby was the most popular and arguably the most talented player in the league. General manager Ray Shero decided to shop for players at the trading deadline who could help in the post-season. The first player Shero grabbed was Gary Roberts from the Florida Panthers. At forty, Roberts was old enough to be Crosby's father. In fact, Roberts was drafted by the Cal-

NHL. He won the Art Ross Trophy as the league's leading scorer with 120 points (36 goals, 84 assists) in 79 games, 6 more than runner-up Joe Thornton from the San Jose Sharks. Crosby also became the youngest Art Ross winner ever. Wayne Gretzky was slightly younger when he tied Marcel Dionne for the NHL lead with 137 points in 1979–80 but Dionne had won the trophy for scoring more goals. Crosby also edged out Gretzky by 140 days to become the youngest player to post 200 career points. Crosby finished his sophomore season with 222 career regular season points, reaching 200 at age 19 years and 207 days. He also showed a flair for clutch play by scoring five game-winning goals. It didn't take long—two seasons in fact—but already Sidney Crosby was excelling in the NHL just as he had in Midget Triple-A, high school, and major junior hockey. His next challenge was the Stanley Cup playoffs.

The Penguins marked their return to the Stanley Cup playoffs with a matchup with the Ottawa Senators in the opening round. Ottawa and Pittsburgh had finished tied during the regular season with 105 points, but the Senators were awarded the higher fourth seed in the overall standings because they had 48 wins to the Penguins' 47. Even though the Senators had home-ice advantage, many expected the Penguins to emerge victorious in the best-of-seven-game series. Pittsburgh had improved dramatically as the season progressed, and expectations were suddenly high for a

Well-Balanced Attack

The Pittsburgh Penguins featured the best player in the league—Sidney Crosby. They also had the top rookie, Evgeni Malkin, with Jordan Staal a close second. But beyond these three players, the 2006–07 edition of the Penguins was balanced, with many other players providing important contributions. These contributions led to a fifth-place finish in the NHL's Eastern Conference and the team's first playoff berth since 2000.

The Pens featured:
- 2 players with at least 30 goals
- 5 players with at least 20 goals
- 11 players with at least 10 goals
- 5 players with at least 10 power play goals
- 7 players with at least 40 points
- 15 players with an even or better plus-minus rating

team that finished 34 points out of a playoff spot just twelve months earlier.

Ottawa was also a team that had steadily improved its performance as the season wound down, but expectations for the Senators were still modest based on previous playoff failures. Ottawa had never had much success in the playoffs, and most hockey pundits were expecting another quick exit. They were wrong.

After splitting the first two games in Ottawa, the Senators won the last three games of the series by a combined score of 9–3, advancing with a four-games-to-

Sidney Crosby battles against the Ottawa Senators in his first playoff series in 2007.

disappointed with the outcome, he was already primed for the next season, when expectations would be much higher for the Penguins. "Looking at the big picture, it was a great season," Michel Therrien said. "We have to be optimistic about the future."

As Therrien, Ray Shero, and the Pittsburgh Penguins players looked to future, they did so with Sidney Crosby leading the way. Already the Pens were "his" team: he was the face of the franchise and by far its best player. Shortly after being eliminated from the playoffs, the team announced Crosby would become the youngest team captain in NHL history. (The Penguins had not had a captain since Mario Lemieux retired in January 2006.) "It is obvious to all of us—coaches, players, management, staff—that [Crosby] has grown into the acknowledged leader of the Pittsburgh Penguins," said Shero. "It is only appropriate that he wears the 'C' as team captain."

The Penguins' organization owed a lot to Crosby, too. On July 10, 2007, less than a month after the NHL awards presentations, the Pittsburgh Penguins announced they had signed Crosby to a five-year contract extension. The new deal runs through the 2012–13 season and will pay number 87 $43.5 million (U.S.), or an average of $8.7 million per season. "That seems like a pretty good number," Crosby, who was born on the seventh day of the eighth month in the year 1987, said during a press conference announcing the deal. "We have a lot of

one opening-round win. In the playoffs, the intense media pressure around Crosby was even brighter. Every game was broadcast nationally on *Hockey Night in Canada*, and it seemed even when Ottawa began dominating the series, the television cameras and commentators focused on Crosby more than any other player. Still, Crosby performed well under the conditions, scoring three goals and adding two assists in the five games he played. "It was a big turnaround," explained Crosby. "The playoffs were tough, but maybe it was something that had to happen for us to learn." While

Sidney Crosby posing with his trophies at the NHL Awards Gala in 2007.

On June 14, 2007, with the Anaheim Ducks still celebrating their Stanley Cup victory, the stars of the National Hockey League gathered in Toronto for the league awards ceremony. Several storylines emerged that night, including Martin Brodeur from the New Jersey Devils winning his second consecutive Vezina Trophy as the NHL's top goalie, and Crosby teammate Evgeni Malkin taking home the Calder Trophy. But the night, and most of the hardware, belonged to Sidney Crosby. As the NHL's scoring leader, he was awarded the Art Ross Trophy. He also took home the Pearson Trophy as the NHL's Most Valuable Player, as voted on by members of the National Hockey League's Players' Association.

The evening ended with the presentation of the Hart Trophy as the MVP of the NHL, and again Crosby was called to the podium to accept the honour. It was a record-setting night for the nineteen-year-old, as he became the youngest player ever to win each of these major awards. "The fans love him," Brodeur said. "Everybody seems to be on his wagon, and that's well deserved. He's going to be like Gretzky in making the NHL a better sport."

Just four years after playing for Nova Scotia at the 2003 Canada Winter Games in northern New Brunswick, Crosby was the most famous and arguably the best hockey player in the world. As he accepted the Hart Trophy, Crosby used the moment to thank his parents, sitting in the audience. "The sacrifices of my parents, the early mornings, the practices," Crosby said. "I owe a lot of thanks to them."

young guys and hopefully over the next six years we can all grow together," Crosby told CTV News as he took a break from a training session at the Cole Harbour Place fitness facility. "I think Ray [Shero] has talked a lot about keeping that core together and we've made a lot of steps to do that. It's nice to know I'll be with those guys."

Crosby's fame extended outside the hockey world, too. He had quickly become one of the most recognized celebrities in North America, and his name was aligned with some major corporations. By the time he turned twenty years old, Crosby was endorsing Gatorade and Reebok, and in August 2007 he released his own line of clothing, a collaboration with Reebok and SportChek. When the line was unveiled in Toronto, Crosby admitted he actually sat down with designers and offered his opinion on certain colours and styles. "It was the last thing I'd imagine myself doing. But we had fun with it." Crosby was also featured on the covers of *GQ*, *Vanity Fair*, and *Time* magazines, and in January 2008 he was number one on the *Hockey News* top 100 list of people of power and influence in hockey, the first time a player, and not an executive, was named to the top spot.

A new long-term contract, a young competitive team to grow with, a new arena on the horizon, a "C" on his sweater, and a mantel laden with three new major awards. It took just two seasons, but Sidney Crosby and his Penguins were on their way. At one time he was just a promising prospect on a last-place hockey team. But now he was a superstar on one of the better organizations in the NHL.

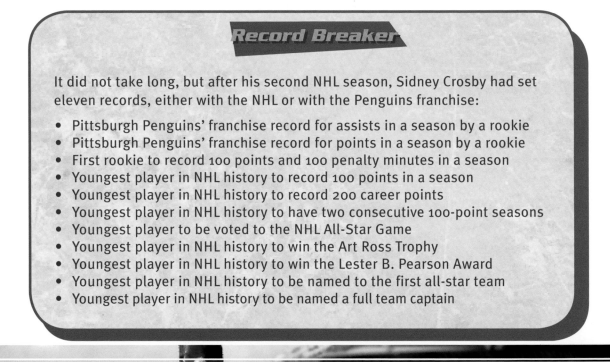

Record Breaker

It did not take long, but after his second NHL season, Sidney Crosby had set eleven records, either with the NHL or with the Penguins franchise:

- Pittsburgh Penguins' franchise record for assists in a season by a rookie
- Pittsburgh Penguins' franchise record for points in a season by a rookie
- First rookie to record 100 points and 100 penalty minutes in a season
- Youngest player in NHL history to record 100 points in a season
- Youngest player in NHL history to record 200 career points
- Youngest player in NHL history to have two consecutive 100-point seasons
- Youngest player to be voted to the NHL All-Star Game
- Youngest player in NHL history to win the Art Ross Trophy
- Youngest player in NHL history to win the Lester B. Pearson Award
- Youngest player in NHL history to be named to the first all-star team
- Youngest player in NHL history to be named a full team captain

chapter five

Chasing the Cup

I f the 2006–07 season and the early playoff exit at the hands of the Ottawa Senators was part of the learning curve required for a young team on the rise, then the next season was an opportunity for the Pittsburgh Penguins to elevate their play to a new level. "It was obviously a tough finish," Crosby said in the moments following the 3–0 loss to the Senators in game five of the opening-round, quarter-final series. "But I think we exceeded a lot of expectations in the regular season and we'll have to learn from this."

The Penguins soon made it clear that they had learned a lot from their brief playoff experience. But before the young team was completely on track, there would be several low points in the early portion of the season, surprising slumps, adversarial moments, a major injury, and another Crosby milestone—his first NHL fight.

On December 20, 2007, the Penguins were playing the Bruins in Boston. With fifteen minutes to go in the second period, Bruins defenseman Andrew Ference finished his check and rode Crosby into the boards to the left of Boston goalie

Sidney Crosby and Sergei Gonchar celebrate an overtime goal in 2008.

Tim Thomas. Crosby had been hit hard many times in his junior and NHL career, but this time he reacted with surprising aggression. Before Crosby had regained his balance, both players had their gloves off and a fight ensued. Crosby landed six quick punches, took half as many, and after a brief struggle he landed underneath Ference as both players fell to the ice. When he got up and skated to the penalty box, the 15,304 fans in attendance at the roared their approval for Ference. It was Crosby's first fight and first career major penalty.

Why did Crosby react the way he did? One obvious reason was frustration. The Penguins were slumping. In

that game against the Bruins, they let a 4–0 lead slip away, before hanging on for a 5–4 shootout victory. After the game Crosby swatted away any suggestions that he was unveiling a new element to his NHL game. "I don't think so," Crosby replied when asked if fans and media should expect to see him fight more often. "It's not going to be something I make a habit of by any means."

For Pierre McGuire, one of the secrets to understanding Crosby as a person and competitor is to appreciate the level of intensity he brings to the arena every game. That first fight against Ference was a glimpse, and McGuire says there are other examples. "The thing some people don't know about Sidney is he's also extremely intense," said McGuire. "I was working at ice level for a Penguins game on NBC versus the Rangers and he got hit in the mouth by Scott Gomez. The TV timeout came and during the commercial he came over to me and was yelling and said 'Pierre did you say I embellished this?' He showed his mouth guard and the black tape from Gomez's stick had left a black smudge. He was furious. He brings that intensity to every game."

In the early portion of the 2007–08 season, anyway, Crosby's intensity was not translating into wins for his team. On

December 21, 2007, the Penguins lost 4–2 to the New York Islanders, dropping their record to a surprisingly mediocre 17–16–2. "We have to be better," said Crosby after the game. Two days later, they were better, and the team broke out of its slump and started an eight-game winning streak. The winning streak came to an end on January 18, 2008, with a home ice 3–0 shootout loss to the Tampa Bay Lightning. More importantly, not only did the Penguins lose the game, they lost their captain to a long-term injury. In the first period, Tampa Bay's Paul Ranger slashed Crosby, sending him feet first into the boards. When he attempted to get up, Crosby limped and had to be helped off the ice.

The post-game diagnosis confirmed a high ankle sprain. "When I saw him leave the ice, I got the feeling it was very severe," head coach Michel Therrien said. "There is no team that can deal with losing the best player in the league. He is the heart of the team and he is our leader. We are going to face adversity and we are going to have to battle through it."

At the time of the injury, Crosby was the NHL's leading scorer with 63 points in 46 games. Losing their best player during a season already fraught with inconsistency seemed to be a devastating blow for the Penguins. But after the game in which Crosby was injured, Tampa Bay Lightning forward Vincent Lecavalier offered a prophetic assessment of the situation facing the Penguins. "Sid is a big part of that team. For

In His Own Words

"I was fortunate to grow up in the Maritimes and be brought up the way my parents did. And the [people in the] community think of you as a brother or a sister and that means a lot to me. Sidney Crosby is carrying the torch now, and the kids in the Maritimes are very fortunate to have a person like him—not just a hockey player—to look up to. He carries himself very well and he's a friendly, easygoing guy. He just has this special gift that he's the best player in the world. Tell everyone to enjoy it because that doesn't come around every day, and there might not be another player like him for another thirty or forty years."

GLEN MURRAY
Former NHL forward,
in an interview with the *Halifax Chronicle Herald*

them to win, someone else is going to have to lead, and I think Evgeni Malkin is going to have to do that."

Malkin would in fact lead the Penguins to unexpected prosperity. When Crosby injured his ankle against Tampa Bay, the Penguins had 25 wins in 44 games. Not a poor performance, but hardly dominating, and one that had only just been boosted by an eight-game winning streak. In the ten games following the injury, Pittsburgh would lose just

It is difficult to capture the pride that Cole Harbour residents feel toward Sidney Crosby. Take a drive through the town and you'll see those two signs, erected by the Halifax Regional Municipality, inscribed "Welcome to Cole Harbour" and "Home of Sidney Crosby." Drive by Colonel John Stuart Elementary School at recess in the morning, and you'll bear witness to dozens of children wearing Pittsburgh Penguins number 87 jerseys, hats, and T-shirts. Within a twenty-kilometre radius of Crosby's boyhood home there are touching reminders everywhere that this is more than a stellar hockey player. He's an adored human being. What he does, who he is, and how he carries himself matter to his hometown fans. Cheering for home-grown heroes is nothing new, but the relationship between Nova Scotia hockey fans and Crosby seems to have an extra layer of texture.

Crosby's former coach from the Midget AAA Dartmouth Subways reads it this way: "He's a blue collar guy which everyone around here appreciates," said Brad Crossley. "Sidney doesn't like to talk about his paycheque. He's a very humble guy...and he's not boastful. And he approaches the game like he's a fourth line player trying to make an impact. That's the way he trains and plays." Clearly the way Crosby plays holds particular appeal for Cole Harbour residents. During the 2008 Stanley Cup final against Detroit, more than a thousand fans crammed Cole Harbour Place to watch the *Hockey Night in Canada* broadcast on several big screen televisions. These fans may not have gone home happy at the end of game six, but they did send a resounding message that they were behind him every step of the way. They proved it in the spring of 2008. They would do it again twelve months later.

two games in regulation. On March 16, with Crosby still nursing the injury, the Penguins pounded the Philadelphia Flyers 7–1, paced by Malkin's two goals and two assists.

The Penguins were still Sidney Crosby's team, and he was still their most decorated player, but the Penguins were serving notice that this team was not one-dimensional. The injury to Crosby had forced other key players to elevate their play with the Stanley Cup playoffs

quickly approaching. "Geno [Malkin]... for whatever reason, seems to turn it up a notch when Sid's not in the lineup. I can't really explain why," said defenseman Brooks Orpik. Philadelphia head coach John Stevens agreed: "Malkin may be the best player in the league right now, and you have to respect that fact."

On March 4, Crosby returned to the Penguins' lineup after missing 21 games with the ankle injury. In his absence the Penguins had a 11–6–4 record. On this night their opponent was the same team they played on the night of the injury, but the result was different: The Penguins won 2–0 and Crosby showed little rust from the long layoff by notching two assists. "It's good to get it over with and get that feel and get that tim-

ing back, but it's still not there," Crosby said after the game. "I had some great chances that I would have loved to put in. It didn't happen. Sometimes that's the way it goes. I'm a little rusty."

The Penguins would continue to cruise through the remainder of the regular season, finishing second in the Eastern Conference with 102 points, two back of the top-seed Montreal Canadiens.

For the first three rounds of the playoffs, Pittsburgh was relatively unchallenged. The Pens swept Ottawa in four games in the opening round, and then followed with series victories against the New York Rangers and the Philadelphia Flyers, both in five games. Crosby had 21 points in 14 games (4 goals, 17 assists) to

Sidney Crosby scores against Vesa Toskala and the Toronto Maple Leafs.

help lift the Penguins to their first Stanley Cup Final appearance since 1992.

The Penguins' run through the Eastern Conference to reach the Stanley Cup was a stunning achievement. Like the Edmonton Oilers teams of the 1980s, the Penguins were highly skilled, improving on what seemed to be a game-by-game basis. The team featured an exciting group of young hockey players who were quickly capturing the imaginations of hockey fans not just in their home city, but also across the North America and around the world.

Often in professional sports, especially the NHL, teams need to go through the experience of losing first before they win. In 1983 the New York Islanders won their fourth consecutive Stanley Cup by sweeping aside the youthful Oilers. There's a famous story about Wayne Gretzky looking into the winning Islanders dressing room after game four and seeing a group of aging, banged-up players, clearly worse for wear based on the punishment they endured to win that fourth and final championship. Gretzky, as the story goes, knew then that he had just received a crash course on the sacrifices needed in order to secure a championship. The Oilers were a dazzling young team filled with future hall-of-famers. Their star players were taking the league and its fans by storm. But they were soft. They were not pushing their play and their bodies to the limit like the Islanders just had. Winning was not easy, and the veteran New York players had just proved how

difficult and physically costly a task it was.

The 2008 Pittsburgh Penguins were by no measure blissfully unaware of their competitive surroundings. Yes they had a lot of young stars, but the Pittsburgh roster was also sprinkled with veteran talent in the form of Hal Gill, Sergei Gonchar, and Gary Roberts. But age and experience were not the only factors in the championship series—history would record that the Detroit Red Wings simply overmatched the Penguins. Detroit would shut down the high-octane Penguins' offence in games one and two with 3–0 and 4–0 victories. The Penguins showed some resilience, winning two of the next four games, but the Red Wings prevailed in six games. If losing was part of the recipe for learning how to win, the Penguins had just received a crash course. Still, conventional wisdom suggested this was a team on the rise. Their head coach said as much in the press conference following game six. "We're going in the right direction with those young kids," said coach Michel Therrien. "The future is bright with those young kids. This is definitely a team that is really fun to coach. They paid a price to try to get better. I'm really proud of my players."

Crosby's post-game reaction was full of the predictable disappointment that goes hand in hand with losing a Stanley Cup Final. What he was feeling (or what we imagine he was feeling) at that moment was captured later in the year in a clever television commercial produced

Sidney Crosby shakes hands with members of the Detroit Red Wings after losing the 2008 Stanley Cup final in six games.

by the NHL. The ad started with a shot of the Penguins players around the team bench, watching the Red Wings in the minutes following the final game. The camera moves to a still photo of Crosby, and play-by-play announcer Mike "Doc" Emrick says, "The Red Wings are the Stanley Cup champions." At that moment, the picture of Crosby transforms into a real life image and he says, "This is a tough one. Getting this close and not winning the Cup. But I know it will make our team even stronger." Crosby then pauses, looks at his teammates, stares up at the Pittsburgh fans in the Mellon Arena, and with an indignant look on his face, addresses the viewer again: "I never want to be in this picture again." The ad series was named "Is this the year?" As the 2008–09 regular season approached, that would remain the key question. Pittsburgh was sure to be very good again, perhaps the top team in the Eastern Conference. But Detroit, among other teams, would also be very good. Crosby and the Penguins would have but one goal: prove to themselves and their opponents that this would be the year.

The ties that bind Sidney Crosby to his native Cole Harbour, Nova Scotia, are strong. It seems that Crosby mentions his Nova Scotia roots every chance he gets during interviews, and in the summer months he returns to the area to spend time with his friends and family. So it should come as no surprise that when he began to achieve fame and fortune he used his influence to give something back to his community—especially the vibrant hockey culture in Cole Harbour. "That's where I started," said Crosby in December 2008. "Luckily for me I played there and I had great people to help me."

One of the first opportunities for Crosby to help the great people in his life came after the 2006–07 NHL season, when he won three major NHL trophies, including the Lester B. Pearson Award as the top NHL player as voted by his peers. "You get twenty thousand dollars with the Pearson trophy to donate back to grassroots community development," said Christi Cooze, a fundraising organizer for Cole Harbour Bel Ayr Minor Hockey Association. "And he chose this organization where he grew up playing hockey." The money was used to support various minor hockey programs, but the most visible impact was new uniforms for the rep competitive teams—each one with a special number 87 crest, a tribute to Cole Harbour's most famous son. "With the opportunity I've had I want to make sure I can do some things," said Crosby. "It's only jerseys and maybe equipment. It's not going to change a kid's life but when I was younger those things really went a long way so I hope it helps out."

When Sidney Crosby gives his time or money to an organization like the Cole Harbour Bel Ayr Minor Hockey Association, he does it because he wants to—because the emotional connection is still intact even after the many years that have passed since he played at Cole Harbour Place. "I'm proud of that. I'm proud to be from [Cole Harbour]," said Crosby. "I have great memories of growing up there with friends. I do whatever I can to help out obviously."

chapter six

Champion

The Pittsburgh Penguins began the 2008–09 regular season as a young team saddled with the burden of high expectations. The team had reached the final quicker than many expected that past June.

Now, players like Crosby, Staal, Malkin, and Fleury were gaining recognition as the core pieces for a team now ready to overcome the final hurdle and bring a Stanley Cup back to western Pennsylvania for the first time since 1992. If the Penguins had been quietly putting together a competitive team throughout the middle part of the decade, they weren't being quiet anymore. The previous June they had a lost the Stanley Cup final to Detroit in a series they could have won. Now, a new season brought with it a new championship opportunity, and most NHL pundits considered the Penguins a legitimate threat to win the Stanley Cup.

After jumping out to a promising start in the 2008–09 regular season, there emerged some early indications that the team's path back to the Stanley Cup final could feature more than a few bumps in the road. In the first half of the season,

Years of futility meant the Penguins had high selections in the NHL Entry Draft. From 2003–2006, a large portion of the Penguins' core was chosen in the opening round of several drafts:

Marc-Andre Fleury—2003
Evgeni Malkin—2004
Sidney Crosby—2005
Jordan Staal—2006

the Penguins were beset by inconsistencies—highs and lows, slumps and winning streaks—and it didn't take long for it to become apparent that the team was not performing to expectations.

On October 30 the Penguins dropped a 4–1 decision to the Phoenix Coyotes. The loss capped a mediocre opening month for the team, which finished with a 5–4–2 record. But the Penguins won nine games in November, and by the time they defeated Carolina 5–2 on December 4, Pittsburgh had a recovered from a sluggish start and sported a 15–6–4 record. But then, the regular season success began to unravel and a perilous two-month slump set in.

On Saturday, February 4, in a game televised on *Hockey Night in Canada*, the Penguins led the Toronto Maple Leafs 2–1 after two periods, only to see Toronto score five straight third-period goals. Pittsburgh lost 6–5. The loss was Pittsburgh's twentieth defeat in thirty-two games and dropped the team five points out of the eighth and final playoff spot in the NHL's Eastern Conference. "It's up to the players," coach Michel Therrien said after the game. "There's a price to pay to win games on the road and right now we're having a hard time staying focused and executing."

Clearly Penguins' general manager Ray Shero felt the same way. Just seven months after Therrien had led his team to the Stanley Cup Final, he was fired and replaced with Dan Bylsma—a former NHL player coaching Pittsburgh's American League farm team. "I didn't like…the direction the team was headed in," Shero said after giving Therrien the news. "I've watched for a number of weeks and, at the end of the day, the direction is not what I wanted to have here. I wasn't comfortable, and that's why the change was made."

The Penguins had lost seven of eight games before the firing, and it appeared the players were no longer responding to Therrien's defensive style of coaching. Bylsma, the new head coach, wasted little time implementing a new up-tempo style of play with players like Sidney Crosby leading the way. "With the strengths we have, we should be able to go into buildings and make teams deal with the quality of players we have at every position," Bylsma said. "I look at a group that can win games right now, and we need to do that. We can do this, but the players have to believe we can do this."

The players responded. The team went 18–3–4 down the stretch to finish in fourth place in the Eastern Conference, good enough for home-ice advantage in the opening round of the playoffs against the Philadelphia Flyers.

Individually, two Penguins, Crosby and Malkin, finished superb seasons. In the end, Crosby finished third in the scoring race with 103 points, seven points behind second-place finisher Alex Ovechkin, and ten behind teammate and overall leader Malkin. It was yet another scoring title for a member of the Pittsburgh Penguins. Mario Lemieux, Jaromir Jagr, and Crosby had combined to win twelve scoring titles with Pittsburgh since 1988. "It's amazing. It really is when you look back at our team's history," said Crosby. "Geno's (Malkin) a well-deserving scoring champion with the way he's played all year. He's been so consistent and so important to our team, so to have it stay in Pittsburgh is great for everybody."

The Penguins had not only survived a tumultuous regular season, but they were now the hottest team in the NHL heading into the playoffs. In addition to the high-scoring Crosby and Malkin, Jordan Staal had finished with 49 points—giving the team perhaps the best depth at the centre position in the NHL. There were other factors that had positioned the team well for another Stanley Cup run: Right wing Bill Guerin, a veteran of more than one thousand NHL career games, was acquired at the trade deadline, and in addition to contributing 12 points in 19 games, he also added key leadership to a dressing room crammed with twenty-something players. Just as importantly, defenseman Sergei Gonchar was back and healthy. A key to Pittsburgh's power play, Gonchar had missed Pittsburgh's first 57 games with an injury, but played an important role in the team's turnaround with 19 points in the final 25 games.

If adversity is a necessary evil for teams to overcome before they can win, then these Pittsburgh Penguins were ready. In ten short months they had fallen short in a six-game Stanley Cup Final, survived a horrific mid-season slump, overcome injuries to their star players, and replaced a head coach. Despite a less-than-dominant regular season, they appeared poised for another shot at a championship.

EASTERN CONFERENCE QUARTERFINAL

For the second straight playoff season, the Penguins faced their Pennsylvania rivals, the Philadelphia Flyers. The series went a bit longer than the previous April, when the Penguins won in five games, but the outcome was the same—a Penguins victory, this time in six games. In the final game of the series, Pittsburgh rallied from a 3–0 deficit to win 5–3.

Sidney Crosby called it a building block for what the team hoped to achieve, especially considering the way the Penguins came back in the final game. Crosby scored the tying goal in the second period and added an empty-net goal in the final minute, capping an eight-point series. "We've had huge rivalries over the years," Crosby said afterward. "It's a loud building. They were playing well and the crowd was into it, so to hear a little silence was gratifying."

Eastern Conference Semifinal

From the moment the two stars broke into the NHL in 2005, considerable debate waged over who was the better player: Sidney Crosby or Alexander Ovechkin? Early in his career, especially following his breakout sophomore season, Crosby was widely considered to be the better of the two players, although by the slightest of margins. But in the following seasons, there was a creeping sense that Ovechkin had surpassed his Pittsburgh counterpart. Now, in the second round of the 2009 Stanley Cup Playoffs, the two players and their respective teams would meet head-to-head.

Adding to the drama was the fierce rivalry the two teams had developed. In fact, Sidney Crosby was not a popular player in the Capitals' dressing room.

"Around the league, a lot of players like Sidney," said TSN's Pierre McGuire. "It may be the Crosby-Ovechkin rivalry or the fact that the Penguins have won more than the Capitals, but either way, he's not liked by that team."

These feelings would make for an entertaining series that featured several shifts in momentum. In the opening game, Washington won 3–2 and both Crosby and Ovechkin scored, but the game was decided on a third-period goal by role player Tomas Fleischmann and by rookie goalie Semyon Varlamov, who stopped 34 shots.

Game two will go down in hockey history as one of the greatest battles between the two superstars. Both Ovechkin and Crosby scored hat tricks—Crosby's in a losing cause as Washington grabbed a 2–0 lead in the best-of-seven series. After the game both players acknowledged that their elevated performances resulted in a memorable playoff game.

"Sick game. Sick three goals by me and Crosby," said Ovechkin. "It's unbelievable to see how fans react, how fans go crazy. The atmosphere right now, it's unbelievable in town."

"It's nice to score," Crosby said. "But it's better to win. I'm sure it's entertaining for people to watch, if I were to look at it from a fan's point of view. As a player, you don't like when the guy on the other team gets a hat trick. That's usually not a good sign."

Journalists can make mistakes—sometimes factual errors, other times they rush to judgement when

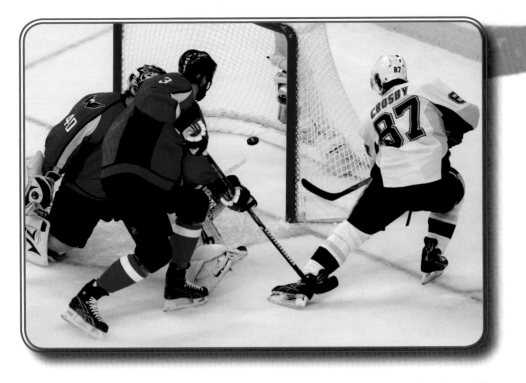

attempting an editorial assessment. In the case of ESPN's Scott Burnside, an incorrect evaluation came in his online column posted minutes after Washington's 4–3, game two win. Burnside, and many hockey observers, had the Penguins written off for dead. Before the series, the Penguins and their captain were the ones creating a buzz among NHL fans. Not anymore:

> They chanted, "M-V-P," and hurled their hats onto the ice. And when it was over, when Alex Ovechkin's hat trick had trumped Sidney Crosby's hat trick in a monumental clash of NHL titans, it was hard not to believe we had witnessed a kind of passing of the torch.

Not the torch that defines who the greater player is—that debate might ever rage—but rather the torch that defines which is the greater team in this moment.

In the wake of this terrific, hard-fought 4–3 Washington Capitals victory Monday, it is hard not to view the Capitals, instead of the Pittsburgh Penguins, as suddenly the young darlings of the Eastern Conference, as suddenly the best young hockey team in the game.

There is no record of the Penguins commenting on this report, but what is apparent is that the next five games nullified any notion of the Washington Capitals supplanting the Pittsburgh

Sidney Crosby scores against the Capitals in the 2009 Stanley Cup Playoffs. The exciting series went the full seven games.

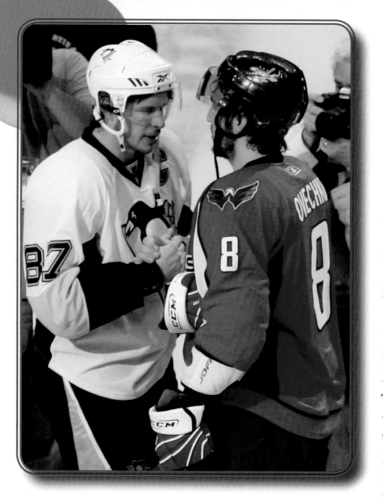

Sidney Crosby and Alexander Ovechkin moments after the Penguins eliminated the Capitals four-games-to-three in the 2009 Stanley Cup Playoffs.

on the surface one could say the Penguins came within an unlucky bounce or two from losing to the Capitals. But in the spirit of Pierre McGuire's mantra that "big name players elevate their play in big games," Sidney Crosby emerged as one such "big-game player." It wasn't that Ovechkin played poorly—14 points in 7 games is hardly a dismal performance—but Crosby, even more than Ovechkin, seemed able to play his best hockey when his team needed it most. In game three, with the Capitals leading the series 2–0, Crosby was on the ice for 28:32 and had two key assists to help his team win 3–2 in overtime and get back into the series. In the winner-take-all game seven, it was Crosby who scored first and set the tone for Pittsburgh to win the game in a convincing fashion. There is no official statistic for a player who displays sheer determination to do what needs to be done at the most important time, but it was Crosby who was most able to seize the moment. He and his Penguins were tested by the Capitals. But they passed every test.

Crosby's performance against the Capitals was historic. He finished with 13 points in 7 games and 8 in the last 5 when the team was making its comeback. The image of Crosby shaking hands with Ovechkin was more than a gentlemanly greeting after a hard-fought series. It was a symbolic achievement. Faced with his greatest challenge in his NHL career, Crosby had succeeded and he and his team appeared to have the wind at their backs as they moved forward in the post-

Penguins as "the best young hockey team in the game." Pittsburgh would win four of the next five games, and the Penguins advanced to their second straight conference final with a 4–3 series victory. In the seventh and deciding game, the Penguins won in a blowout on Washington's home ice, a convincing 6–2 win—paced by Crosby's two goals and one assist.

Pittsburgh's comeback in the series will long be remembered, and was a pivotal moment in their playoff run. Three games in the series went to overtime, so

season. There was no torch being passed; it was more subtle than that. Crosby had outperformed his rival in a crucial playoff series, plain and simple. Ovechkin and Crosby had been neck-and-neck in point totals all season (and likely will be for years to come), but in this Stanley Cup playoff series, Crosby had clearly bested Ovechkin. The Penguins won because Crosby, their best player, had played his best hockey.

"In my opinion, [Crosby's the] best all-around player in the league. He proved it tonight, and no disrespect to any player," Pittsburgh G. M. Ray Shero said after game seven. "Alex Ovechkin is unbelievable for our game. Unbelievable player. But tonight was a statement. Both ends of the ice, Crosby was the best player out there and made it happen for us and said what he is as a player and a person tonight."

The Eastern Conference Final would prove to be an anti-climax for Crosby and the Penguins. Pittsburgh swept the Carolina Hurricanes in four straight games to advance to the Stanley Cup Final for the second straight year—and for the second straight year their opponent would be the Detroit Red Wings.

2009 Stanley Cup Final— Red Wings vs. Penguins, Part II

Since joining the NHL in 1967, the Pittsburgh Penguins have seen both extreme highs and extreme lows. Before Mario Lemieux came to the team in 1984 after being selected first overall in the NHL Entry Draft, the Penguins were known more for losing than winning. In the sixteen years before Lemieux's rookie season, Pittsburgh had missed the playoffs seven times and had never advanced past the second round of the playoffs. Lemieux and the players that the Penguins surrounded him with changed that. Beginning in 1989, Pittsburgh qualified for the post-season in twelve of thirteen years, the highwater mark for the franchise coming in 1991 and 1992, when the Penguins won consecutive Stanley Cups. In 1993, a third straight championship appeared to be within their grasp. But in the Prince of Wales Conference semifinal, the Penguins were upset in seven games by the New York Islanders. At the time, the loss to the Islanders was considered to be nothing more than a minor speed bump for the Penguins dynasty. With the likes of Lemieux, Kevin Stevens, Ron Francis, Larry Murphy, Jaromir Jagr, and Tom Barrasso, the Penguins seemed capable of two and perhaps even three more Stanley Cups.

But it didn't happen. Injuries, retirements, and several more heartbreaking playoff setbacks meant the franchise went into a downward slide. By 2005, the year the Penguins selected Sidney Crosby first overall, the team had missed the playoffs for three straight seasons and were playing many of their home games in a half-empty Mellon Arena. Soon, though, players like Crosby,

The number 87 is now part of the Sidney Crosby brand. Consider the following: In addition to his birthday being the eighth month and seventh day, he also wears the number 87 and makes an average salary of $8.7 million per season. And when the Penguins defeated the Red Wings 2–1 to win the 2009 Stanley Cup, it was the eighty-seventh game of the 2009 NHL playoffs.

Malkin, and Staal, among others, had once again made the Penguins relevant in Pittsburgh. The NFL's Steelers were still the most popular of the three major sports franchises in the city, but the Penguins, with their young stars and a packed arena, had narrowed the gap. Now, just three years after finishing the regular season with a measly 58 points, the Penguins were back in the Stanley Cup final for the second straight season. The team was only four wins removed from bringing the Stanley Cup back to western Pennsylvania.

Just like the previous season, the Red Wings were fast out of the gate in the 2009 Stanley Cup, winning the first two games by identical 3–1 scores and holding Crosby pointless. Following the second game, with the series shifting to Pittsburgh for games three and four, Crosby wasn't exactly buoyant, but he also was not completely displeased with his team's effort. Unlike the year before, Crosby felt his team played well enough to win both games. "It's not good," Crosby said, "but at the same time, it shows us our game can be successful. If we keep playing the same way, we're going to come out on the right side of things. We would have liked to have different results, but that's playoff hockey."

Crosby was correct to have confidence in his team. And typical of the historic patterns of playoff hockey, being down 2–0 did not necessarily mean the Penguins were without vital signs. In game three Sergei Gonchar broke a 2–2 midway through the third period, lifting his team to an eventual 4–2 victory. Crosby assisted on Gonchar's power play marker, and after the game he talked about the leadership of the Penguins' Russian defenceman who helped his team cut the Detroit series lead in half: "He's a calming influence. He's calm no matter the situation."

That calming influence helped Crosby even further in game four as he scored his first goal of the series in another 4–2 win to pull even with Detroit at two games apiece. The teams traded wins in games five and six, setting the stage for a deciding seventh game to be played at Joe Louis Arena in Detroit on June 12.

STANLEY CUP FINAL: GAME SEVEN—JUNE 12, 2009

Heroes come in many forms. At almost every juncture since the NHL lockout ended in 2005, the Pittsburgh Penguins had been led by either Sidney Crosby or Evgeni Malkin. Other players like Jordan Staal and Sergei Gonchar had also made contributions to the rebuilding project in Pittsburgh, but the stalwarts had been the two top-line centres. But in the deciding game against the Red Wings, it was fourth-line centre Maxime Talbot who led his team with two second-period goals to put the Penguins up 2–0.

While Talbot was playing one of the best games of his career, Crosby was missing a great part of the most important game of *his* career. He was on the bench, unable to play. After leaving the ice late in the second period following a hit by Johan Franzen, Crosby played just one more shift and watched the tense moments of the third period from the sidelines. In the moments following the game, Crosby said the knee injury was not a long-term concern, but the pain he suffered following the hit along the boards made skating and competing against the defending champions an impossibility. "It was so painful, being a captain and seeing what the guys are doing out there blocking shots," Crosby said. "You get to the point where you've got to ask yourself whether you're going to be hurting your team by being out there. I knew I had everything I could

to numb it or try to play through it. At the same time, I'm playing against Pavel Datsyuk and Henrik Zetterberg. One misstep and I could cost the guys a lot of hard work. I didn't want to be the guy who did that."

So with their captain watching from the bench, the Penguins persevered. The Red Wings were playing as if the ice were tilted in their offensive direction. After scoring midway through the third period, Detroit continued to press hard and dominate the Penguins, who were blocking shots, clearing the puck, making saves—doing everything they could to maintain their 2–1 lead. The game came down to the final seconds. Goaltender Marc-André Fleury—just a few days after losing 5–0 in game five—made an incredible, last-second diving save on Nicklas Lidstrom, and the game was over. The Penguins mobbed their goaltender, celebrating the gut-wrenching, championship-clinching win. "I knew there wasn't much time left," Fleury said. "The rebound was wide. I just decided to get my body out there and it hit me in the ribs so it was good." Pittsburgh had captured the team's first Stanley Cup championship in seventeen years.

For all the exploits of Talbot and Fleury, Crosby was the guy who got to hoist the Stanley Cup first. Knee injury or not, Crosby was on the ice for the historic moment when NHL commissioner Gary Bettman presented him with the trophy. It was a moment many around the NHL had expected for some

ship. "It's a dream come true," Crosby said. "It's everything you imagined and more. I would've loved to do it in four [games]. It would have been a lot easier on the nerves."

The end of the game was not without controversy. When the Red Wings lined up to shake hands with the Penguins, Crosby was delayed by interviews with NBC and CBC. The result: some of the Detroit players, including captain Nicklas Lidstrom, did not have the chance to congratulate the Penguins captain, leading to some harsh criticism levelled at Crosby. "Nick was waiting and waiting, and Crosby didn't come over to shake his hand. That's ridiculous, especially as their captain," said Red Wings forward Kris Draper.

Crosby later responded to the accusation: "I just won the Stanley Cup. I think I have the right to celebrate with my teammates. I know it's not easy waiting around...I understand if they don't feel like waiting around. But you know what? It's the easiest thing to do in the world, to shake hands after you win. I had no intentions of trying to skip guys and not shake their hands. I think that was a pretty unreasonable comment."

Sidney Crosby shares the 2009 Stanley Cup with his Pittsburgh teammates.

time. Four years after being drafted first overall by the Penguins, the player many had tabbed to be the next dominant superstar had reached the pinnacle of NHL success before his twenty-second birthday, and was the youngest captain in NHL history to win the champion-

THE CUP COMES TO COLE HARBOUR

Sidney Crosby was a Stanley Cup champion. On June 15 the city of Pittsburgh hosted a parade for the champion Pen-

guins, and tens of thousands of fans lined the streets of the city to celebrate (just five months after the Steelers had held a Super Bowl parade following their sixth NFL championship). Crosby was the star attraction at the celebration, and he brought his parents, Troy and Trina, along.

"We want to go for more," Crosby told the screaming crowd. "I just want to say it was a privilege and an honour to go through this with everyone. We've all dreamed of doing this, and let's do it again some other time."

Now, Crosby was returning home to share the championship with his family, friends, and fellow Nova Scotians. One of those friends was Paul Mason, a for-mer peewee hockey and Little League baseball coach who had stayed in close contact with the Crosby family over the years. "The day after he won the Stanley Cup, his mom and dad called and Sidney was there too," Mason said. "They said we have a favour to ask of you. We want a parade of some kind. Would you or-ganize something for us? I said sure and it began…a very busy summer. It was a phenomenal and rewarding experience."

It was also an experience that would feature Sidney Crosby's direct input. Ac-cording to Mason, Crosby wanted the one-day celebration to touch not just the streets of his neighbourhood—he wanted it to be a reflection of the fond-ness he felt for the province as a whole

Sidney Crosby lifts the Stanley Cup on the streets of Pittsburgh as the city celebrates its 2009 Stanley Cup champions.

eighth month in 1987—thus the number on his jersey, 87. So Crosby's Stanley Cup celebration would also be a birthday celebration—and thousands of Maritimers would be on hand for the party.

On the morning of August 7, 2009, a Sea King helicopter bearing Sidney Crosby and the Stanley Cup landed on HMCS *Preserver*. Thousands of fans waited dockside for their first glimpse of the Penguins captain on what would likely be one of the busiest days of his life. It was a layered celebration, a rollout that included political leaders, friends, former coaches, current and ex-teammates, and Canada's military. "You know it's almost like a dream. You don't even think it's really you," said Crosby, moments after landing on the *Preserver*. "I never would have thought I'd be in a helicopter, getting ready to land on a navy ship and share it with all the servicemen and women here."

After signing autographs for fans and members of the military and their families, Crosby and the Stanley Cup were ushered off to a private visitation at the IWK Health Centre to meet

Minister of National Defence Peter MacKay looks on as Sidney Crosby carries the Stanley Cup onto HMCS *Preserver* **on Sidney Crosby Day, August 7, 2009.**

and the people living in it. "When I met with him and talked to him about how it would go, he already had a set idea of how it would go with every detail. He wanted to go to the hospital and meet with the kids. He wanted the ground hockey game with his friends. There was never any question that it would be based out of his home community of Cole Harbour."

He also had a date in mind. Crosby was born on the seventh day of the

with children who were patients at the hospital. From there it was off to his native Cole Harbour for a Stanley Cup parade, attended by thousands. As the August sunshine beat down on the crowd, Crosby slowly worked his way toward Cole Harbour Place—the athletic facility where Crosby had played his minor hockey. He took to a stage with his Pittsburgh teammate Maxime Talbot and answered dozens of questions from fans of all ages. After a street hockey game in which Crosby played goalie, he held a private party at his house—and then the next morning it was over.

The Stanley Cup was leaving Nova Scotia, but not before the province's most famous citizen had gone to great lengths and effort to share his moment of ultimate success with his peers. "He really showed that he's not just a great hockey player," said Jonathan Walsh, one of the thousands of fans who lined the streets of Cole Harbour for the parade. "I think he's a great ambassador to the country."

His former midget coach, Brad Crossley, one of Crosby's inner circle

who was invited to the private post-parade party, said the entire occasion was just another example of how his former player was more than a great hockey player—he was also a tremendously generous, gracious, and accommodating human being. "Prior to him coming to us he just had special gifts. He's an outstanding individual and I think that's what we're more proud of here in Nova Scotia."

Sidney Crosby signs his name to support Canadian troops overseas, August 7, 2009.

**Sharing
the Stanley
Cup with a
huge crowd
on Halifax's
waterfront,
August 7,
2009.**

In just twenty-four hours the celebration in Cole Harbour was over. Crosby was now twenty-two years old. After two months of speculation and anticipation, Cole Harbour's favourite son had returned the prodigal hero, basking in the glow of his Stanley Cup win. He was the youngest captain in NHL history to win the Stanley Cup, and he would now have six weeks of summer left to prepare for a new season. On the road to the defence of the Stanley Cup, Crosby would also play a central role in another title quest—and this one would be Olympic in proportion.

chapter seven

The Golden Goal

The 2009–10 NHL season began with high expectations for the Pittsburgh Penguins. They were the defending champions, and given that the young nucleus of their team was still largely intact, many hockey prognosticators picked the Penguins to repeat as Stanley Cup victors.

It has been written and said many times before: successfully defending a Stanley Cup championship has been more difficult than winning the championship in the first place. But it seemed the only thing that could possibly hold the Penguins back was complacency and fatigue. With 2010 an Olympic year, the NHL would shut down for almost three weeks as hockey's best players travelled to Vancouver to represent their respective countries in the 2010 Winter Olympics. After playing into the beginning of June and enjoying a short summer, the Penguins' top players would have more high-level hockey to play in the middle of a gruelling NHL regular season.

That Crosby would play for Team Canada at the Olympics was never in question. The official announcement of his selection would come on December 30—but well

Carrying the Olympic flame through the streets of Halifax, November 18, 2009.

before that announcement, when the Olympic Torch Relay rolled through Crosby's home province, he was the star attraction. The torch relay passed through hundreds of communities all over the country, but when it made its way through Halifax, Crosby was there.

Crosby's turn to hoist the Olympic flame came on November 18, sandwiched between a game against Anaheim on the 16th and a road game in Ottawa on the 19th. Getting away for just a few hours to visit Nova Scotia on such an historic occasion meant an interlude in the middle of an already busy schedule, but according to Crosby, this was a trip

home he was not going to pass up. "I am honoured and thrilled to have the opportunity to carry the Olympic flame in my home province of Nova Scotia," Crosby said in a release. "The torch relay will pass through so many communities and hands on the way to Vancouver and I'm privileged to be part of that special group as the Olympic Flame makes its way to Vancouver for the 2010 Winter Games."

It came as little surprise that Halifax's downtown was basically cordoned off for the entire day on the 18th—necessary to accommodate the huge crowd that was expected to be on hand. There was no official head count—estimates put the crowd anywhere from fifteen to thirty thousand—but Brunswick Street was packed with people.

As Crosby reached the handoff point with snowboarder Sarah Conrad, the crowd that had lined the sidewalk converged on him and the security team running alongside. By the time Crosby finished his portion of the relay, he was wearing what could only be described as a look of considerable concern. As he slipped past the crowd, he scampered into the Halifax Metro Centre–World Trade and Convention Centre facility for a press conference and media interview with TSN (conducted by this author).

"It's a once in a lifetime opportunity," said Crosby. "Who would have thought that I would be somewhat close to Halifax with us travelling to Ottawa with a couple of days in between games. I felt pretty fortunate when they contacted me that I could do this."

While Crosby admitted he was surprised by the size of the crowd, he did say the level of the enthusiasm was what he expected. As he had witnessed during the Stanley Cup celebration three months earlier in August, Crosby knew that the people of the province were now taking what was almost civic pride in his growing list of accomplishments. "I'm always spoiled here by the support," said Crosby. "It's the kind of thing that I experienced with the Stanley Cup parade and tonight wasn't any different. It was incredible to see the turnout along the hill and along the way."

The 2010 Winter Olympics in Vancouver were far from just another Olympic Games—at least from a Canadian point of view. It was, as the organizers had billed it, an opportunity to "Own The Podium" on home soil and win the most medals. Above all, the pressure was on for Canada to win the gold medal in men's hockey. When Canada won the gold in men's hockey in 2002, it ended a fifty-year drought and reaffirmed Canada's position as a hockey power. A disappointing finish at Torino, Italy, in 2006, however, whetted the country's appetite for another finish atop the podium. The desire to win hockey gold on Canadian soil was reaching a fever pitch.

When the tournament began, Canada cruised to an 8–0 win over Norway. With the team's following game against Switzerland, a quality opponent but one Canada was expected to defeat, it seemed things would come together easily for Team Canada. But an early 2–0 lead became 2–2, and the tension on the faces of the Canadian players and fans became evident. It took a Sidney Crosby shootout goal for the team to escape with a too-close-for-comfort 3–2 victory over Switzerland. When Crosby scored the shootout winner, the look on his face was one of sheer intensity, almost anger—anger that what should have been a tune-up game came close to being a historic upset victory by Switzerland. After the game, Crosby admitted his team did not play well. "I wouldn't say [we played well], but the gold-medal game is not tomorrow, so

that's the good news." However, the news would not be so good when Canada played the USA in their final round-robin match. The Canadians lost 5–3 in a game that saw Crosby score his first regulation goal of the tournament. Not good enough for a country known for the pride it places on the achievements of its Olympic hockey teams. As teams began to prepare for the next round, commentators and fans suggested this version of Team Canada had not been put together properly, was not good enough to win the gold medal, and was destined to suffer a similar fate to the Canadian Olympic hockey teams that fell short in Nagano in 1998 and Torino in 2006.

If there was trepidation over Canada's loss to Americans, it was washed away with an 8–2 win over Germany in the qualification round and, especially, by a 7–3 victory over Russia in the quarterfinal. Before the Olympics, Russia had raised more than a few eyebrows by selecting several of their players from the Russian Kontinental Hockey League ahead of Russian-born NHLers. In the quarterfinal game against Canada, it soon became clear that the Russians were not equipped to compete with the Canadians, as the host country's squad dominated the game in all aspects. But it was not the Crosby-Ovechkin matchup that so many would have expected in the weeks leading into the Olympics. Both players were held off the scoresheet, and one (Ovechkin) was heading back to his NHL team after having been denied a chance to win a medal.

Men's Hockey at the 2010 Winter Olympics

FINAL STANDINGS

1. Canada
2. USA
3. Finland
4. Slovakia
5. Sweden
6. Russia
7. Czech Republic
8. Switzerland
9. Belarus
10. Norway
11. Germany
12. Latvia

TEAM CANADA RESULTS

February 16 — Canada 8/Norway 0
February 18 — Canada 3/Switzerland 2 (shootout)
February 21 — USA 5/Canada 3
February 23 — Canada 8/Germany 2
February 24 — Canada 7/Russia 3
February 26 — Canada 3/Slovakia 2
February 28 — Canada 3/USA 2 (OT)

LEADING SCORERS

	games	goals	assists	points
1 Pavol Demitra (SVK)	7	3	7	10
2 Marián Hossa (SVK)	7	3	6	9
3 Zach Parise (USA)	6	4	4	8
4 Brian Rafalski (USA)	6	4	4	8
5 Jonathan Toews (CAN)	7	1	7	8
6 Jarome Iginla (CAN)	7	5	2	7
7 Sidney Crosby (CAN)	7	4	3	7
8 Dany Heatley (CAN)	7	4	3	7
9 Ryan Getzlaf (CAN)	7	3	4	7

In the semifinal, Canada defeated Slovakia 3–2, lifting the team into the gold medal final. The game saw Canada jump out to a 3–0 lead, and then on the strength of Roberto Luongo's 19 saves, the team held on. Despite the team's appearance in the final, there was a lingering sentiment that Sidney Crosby was underperforming at the Olympics. He had been held off the scoresheet in the victories over both Russia and Slovakia and had not delivered a game-altering play since the shootout winner against Switzerland. But that moment would come.

THE GOLD-MEDAL FINAL

Crosby beats USA goalie Ryan Miller to win the gold medal for the Canadian men's hockey team, February 28, 2010.

Canada was not supposed to dominate the men's hockey tournament at the 2010 Winter Olympics, but it was expected to be a serious contender for the gold medal. The opening round was not a failure, but it was hardly a success. A loss to the United States and a strained shootout victory over Switzerland had brought with it a level of unease for the players and hopeful Canadian hockey fans watching across the country.

Teams of destiny always seem to overcome adversity. And Canada men's hockey team was certainly finding its share. In the gold medal final Canada built an early 2–0 lead, only to see the Americans chip away with a goal in the second period and then a last-minute, game-tying marker by Zach Parise. Parise's goal came with the seconds ticking down in the third period. It was an excruciating goal for Canadian fans watching the game across the country. Even the TV cameras were repeatedly showing Team Canada's players standing at the bench, anticipating a gold-medal victory. But Canada had surrendered its two-goal lead and the game was going to overtime. The next goal would win the gold medal.

In the extra period, the teams played four skaters against four, as per International Ice Hockey Federation rules. CTV hockey analyst Pierre McGuire sensed an opportunity for the Canadians. From his vantage point at ice level, he thought Team USA seemed more tired than the Canadians. It had been a long, hard-fought tournament and with two fewer players on the ice for overtime, there would be more area for the remaining players to cover. "You've got Sidney and Jarome Iginla pressing on the forecheck," said McGuire weeks after the Olympics. "I'm saying during the broadcast that fatigue could be a factor for the USA."

In hindsight it was. With the clock ticking toward the eight-minute mark of the first overtime period, the play went to the corner, to the right of USA goaltender Ryan Miller. It didn't seem like a dramatic play was unfolding. There was not the usual thrust of expectation and excitement as is often seen with an odd-man rush, a goal-mouth scramble or a power-play opportunity.

Nevertheless, that's when McGuire saw the definitive battle for the puck, with Sidney Crosby in a critical situation at a critical moment. "Sidney beat Brian Rafalski off the wall," said McGuire. "Watch the highlight closely. Ryan Miller is surprised. His stick is out for the pokecheck, but he left the five-hole exposed and [Crosby] scored."

When it happened—when the goal crossed the line—it seemed like there was a half-second delay, a moment of disbelief followed by a celebration in the corner of Canada Hockey Place. And like a rolling wave, that joyous reaction washed across the entire country.

Sidney Crosby had scored the goal, Canada had won the game, and the Canadians had captured the gold medal. It

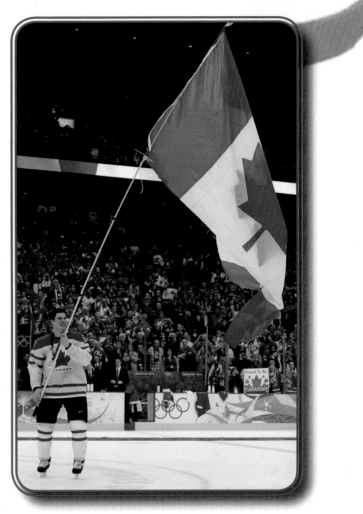

was a moment that brought a country together, a country already basking in the glow of a memorable Olympics. That country was now focussing its adulation on the young man from Cole Harbour, Nova Scotia.

Seven years after he left his home to play high school hockey for Shattuck-St. Mary's in Faribault, Minnesota, and eight months after he had won a Stanley Cup with the Pittsburgh Penguins,

Sidney Crosby celebrates Olympic triumph with an entire nation.

Sidney Crosby had cemented his place in history with one of the biggest goals ever scored for a Canadian national team.

"I had a chance to watch the Paul Henderson goal on TV when I was in grade four," said McGuire. "I was in the studio in 2002 in Salt Lake City and that too was a huge moment. The Crosby goal is a special moment. That was a lifetime moment for all Canadians."

The goal and the celebration that followed brought tremendous satisfaction to a hockey-mad country. But it also marked the release of an enormous pressure point on the Cole Harbour native. If there were lofty expectations for Team Canada, then it was reasonable to assume that players like Crosby—who were tasked with leading the team—felt their weight. Surely he had heard the whispers about the quality of his play in the games leading into the gold-medal final. But once the goal was scored and the Winter Olympics had ended, Crosby returned to the Penguins as a slightly changed man, this according to one of his teammates.

"If the Olympics changed him at all, it relaxed him," Penguins teammate Bill Guerin told *Sports Illustrated* reporter Michael Farber. "Some guys in sports carry the pressure of leading a good team. Some carry the weight of a whole city. He had the weight of a country on his back. The gold was a relief. But with Sid it's like OK, I did it; now let's move on."

The pride felt back in Crosby's old Cole Harbour neighbourhood was profound. Cole Harbour native Jonathan Hughes was driving home from New Orleans when he heard the gold-medal game was going into overtime. So he pulled off the highway in Bangor, Maine, found a sports bar, and witnessed what for him was a special moment in Canadian history.

"[I]t was an intense moment realizing that Sidney Crosby, who went to the same elementary school that I did, scored the winning goal to win gold for Canada. It was amazing," said Hughes the next day. "It's incredible how one person can unite a community and a nation."

chapter eight

Success and Disappointment

After the Olympics, Crosby's next task was to lead the Penguins to another Stanley Cup. The Penguins once again finished strongly in the NHL's Eastern Conference, with 101 points, good enough for fourth place and home-ice advantage in the opening round of the playoffs. From a purely statistical point of view, Crosby had brought the quality of his play to a new level of excellence. His 109 points was not his personal best, but the 51 goals he scored were 12 more than his previous career high, and that number tied him with Steve Stamkos of the Tampa Bay Lightning as the co-winners of the NHL goal scoring title, the Maurice Rocket Richard Trophy.

According to his former midget coach Brad Crossley, Crosby's breakthrough 51 goals were rooted in a decision he made the previous summer to concentrate on improving certain aspects of his game.

"His sponsor changed his sticks this year and he took a little while to get used to them," said Crossley. "He's a got a shooting gallery in his backyard with a fence and

Athletes are sports fans. They may live under a spotlight with fame and riches, but they also appreciate the exploits of other professionals—even those who play other sports. On the night that Crosby returned to the Penguins, the media waited outside the visitors' dressing room at the St. Pete Times Forum. In their midst was New York Yankees outfielder Johnny Damon. Damon took an evening off from the Yankees' spring training schedule to take in a Penguins game and watch the NHL's most famous player. Damon received a hockey stick autographed by Crosby after the pair met in the minutes following the game. "Who's not a fan of Sid?" Damon said. "Seeing that kid play is amazing."

aware Stamkos had scored five goals in his final four games of the season. Winning the Stanley Cup for the second consecutive year remained Crosby's primary goal, but he was not above engaging in some healthy competition with another NHL player. "One of the guys on the bench told me Stamkos had scored," he said. "There's a little bit of healthy competition there and we all know that for the last week or so there has been a bit of a race. I tried to leave it out there and see where it brought me. It's never easy to tie, but I'll take the tie on this one."

Scoring 51 goals was a staggering accomplishment in the eyes of Dennis Potvin, a Hall of Fame defenceman and four-time Stanley Cup champion.

"It tells you a lot about Sidney Crosby," Potvin said on the NHL Network. "Over the summer he said 'I'm going to change my stick pattern a bit and shoot the puck more. I just want to score more goals.' For Sidney Crosby, improving your game a bit means you go and win the Rocket Richard Trophy for most goals in the National Hockey League. He is that kind of player. When this guy puts his mind to something he makes it happen."

a net and he practiced religiously on the ice. Whether it was faceoffs or shooting, he worked on the parts of his game he thought he needed to elevate."

"I worked on shooting the puck this year," admitted Crosby following the Penguins' final game of the regular season against the New York Islanders. Crosby also acknowledged that he was

In previous years, Crosby had been compared to Wayne Gretzky and sometimes Mario Lemieux. After Crosby led the NHL in goals scored, one of his teammates chose a player from another sport as he attempted to draw a parallel. "He's like Michael Jordan," Penguins forward Craig Adams told *Sports Illustrated*. "I don't know how many years it was into Jordan's career, but one day he decides he wants to play defence and goes out and wins the NBA's defensive player award. When Sid puts his mind to something, he can do it."

What he had proven the previous year was that he was capable of leading his team to a Stanley Cup championship. But in 2010, while Crosby would play well at times, the old hockey axiom that suggests it's difficult to repeat as Stanley Cup champions would ring true.

In the opening round, the Penguins lost the first and the fifth games—both on home ice—to the Ottawa Senators, but they made up for it by winning game two and all three games they played in Ottawa. A six-game series victory made it seem as though the Penguins were on the correct course for another playoff run, but the truth was the Ottawa Senators were close to winning the series. Yes, they lost the series, but they played well enough to have won at least two more games.

THE CROSBY HAT TRICK

If there's an unofficial NHL statistic that celebrates players with a combination of toughness and skill, it's the Gordie Howe Hat Trick, accomplished when a player gets a goal, an assist, and has a fight all in the same game. Curiously, Gordie Howe himself only logged two such hat tricks, both against the Toronto Maple Leafs in 1953 and again in 1954. On the night of April 16, 2010,

in game two of the Eastern Conference quarterfinal, Sidney Crosby played one of the most complete and well-balanced games of his career—and when the game had ended he had achieved Howe-like immortality by creating what would later be known as the Crosby Hat Trick: a goal, an assist, and a save.

The goal came in the first period at the 8:45 mark when Crosby crashed the goal crease and scored on a rebound to even the score at 1–1.

The save came with 9:15 left to play in the third and the score still even at one goal apiece. Ottawa defenceman Anton Volchenkov's snapshot beat Penguins goaltender Marc-André Fleury on his trapper side, but as the puck slid toward the goal line, Crosby skated into the goal mouth and flicked the puck away just as it was about to enter the net. Given that Crosby's father, Troy, was a major junior goaltender drafted by the Montreal Canadiens, one could playfully suggest that the Penguins captain has puck-stopping aptitude in his genes. That aside, it was a jaw-dropping play that seemed to quell the Senators' momentum at a critical time. Ottawa had already grabbed a victory in game one of the series in Pittsburgh. A win in game two, with games three and four to be played in Ottawa, would put Pittsburgh in a precarious situation. The goal Crosby stopped from going in the net quite possibly denied Ottawa the game-two win.

The final piece of the Crosby hat trick came with less than five minutes to go in the third period with the score still 1–1. Following a battle along the boards to the left of Ottawa goaltender Brian Elliot, Crosby emerged with the puck and starting skating toward the Ottawa net. Senators' forward Jason Spezza attempted to contain him. Skating behind the icing line, Crosby showcased his puck-protection skills and strength as he skated in large figure eights, with Spezza chasing and attempting to contain him. As Crosby emerged from the net to the left of Brian Elliot, he fell to his knees and while sliding toward the faceoff circle he shovelled to the puck to the blueline. The pass was right onto the stick of Kris Letang, who scored to give the Penguins the lead and the eventual victory.

In addition to dominating Spezza, Crosby also displayed his tenacity—his ability to seemingly change the course of a game by himself. It wasn't just the fact that he was the best player in the game—it was the manner in which he contributed to two key turning points in the game, especially the save and the assist.

Not surprisingly, Crosby's game-two performance was the talk of the sports media throughout the weekend. *Toronto Sun* columnist and TSN contributor Steve Simmons had this to say: "There's nothing to be cynical about anymore with Sidney Crosby. He just keeps getting better and better and better and whatever is inside of him, winning last week didn't matter. He wants to win next week, he wants to win today. He's got that special quality that so few great athletes have. He's getting better with age."

And he had single-handedly changed the momentum of the series. The Crosby Hat Trick was the turning point. "It's impossible to stop him, especially every night," Senators coach Cory Clouston said about Crosby. "He was the best player on the ice and he showed what he is able to do. When they needed a goal, he made a big play."

Given that he totalled a staggering 14 points in the 6 games against Ottawa, it can be safely said there were many stellar moments for Crosby in the series. Game four, when he totalled two goals and two assists, stood out as his best statistical performance. Making the game and the night even more interesting was the reaction of the Ottawa fans. From the moment the puck was dropped at the beginning of the game, they were on Crosby, yelling at him and booing him every time he stepped on the ice. Back in Nova Scotia, Brad Crossley, who was watching the game, listened to the crowd's reaction with amusement, knowing full well that the more they booed Crosby, the better he would perform. "When they were booing Sidney I just said 'Don't do that,'" said Crossley. "That is the worst thing. I've seen it before many times. He'll feed off that and just get better. And he did."

After the Penguins dispatched the Senators, Crosby's next opponent was a surprise entrant into the Stanley Cup playoffs' second round—the Montreal Canadiens. Montreal had just shocked the hockey world by upsetting the top-seed Washington Capitals in

Born to be a champion.

Playmaker to Goal Scorer

Since his NHL career began in 2005, Sidney Crosby has transformed his game. Once thought of primarily as a playmaker, he showed in 2009–2010 that he is a goal scorer too. That year, he reached the fifty-goal plateau for the first time in his career and was a co-winner of the Rocket Richard Trophy as the NHL's leading goal scorer. Final goal totals:

- Sidney Crosby   51
- Steven Stamkos   51
- Alexander Ovechkin 50
- Patrick Marleau   44

seven games. The Canadiens were the team that had drafted Crosby's father almost three decades earlier. And as a boy growing up in Cole Harbour, Sidney's bedroom was always decorated with Montreal pennants, posters, and wallpapers—they were his favourite team. Now, as a twenty-two-year-old, he would face them in another gruelling seven-game series.

One game does not make a series, but when Pittsburgh beat Montreal 6–3 in the opener, it appeared to all observers that the Penguins would be in their comfort zone the entire series. But from that game on, the teams traded victories back and forth until—surprisingly—they were tied 3–3 and headed toward a seventh and deciding game. In that final game, Montreal scored on a power play in the opening minute, built a 4–0 lead, and won 5–2 to eliminate the Penguins four games to three.

Unlike the opening-round series against Ottawa, Crosby was mostly shut down. His series totals: one goal and four assists in seven games. Within minutes of game seven ending, Crosby faced questions regarding his level of fatigue. He had been to the Stanley Cup final in two straight years and had led Canada to a gold medal at the Vancouver Olympics. Had the schedule taken its toll? Was he exhausted? How else could he explain his team's shockingly early exit from the playoffs?

"I'm not going to sit here and complain about playing Stanley Cup finals and Olympic gold-medal games," Crosby said. "That's a good problem to have and you have to deal with it. There are times when it is a grind and you have to deal with it. By no means is that any excuse or any reason for anything."

There was some symmetry to the seventh game and its outcome. Back in October of 1967, Montreal beat the expansion Penguins in Pittsburgh in the team's first-ever NHL game. Forty-three years later, the Mellon Arena was now closing its doors and once again the historic occasion was marked by a Montreal victory over Pittsburgh. Still, one can be sure Crosby didn't care too much about Mellon Arena history or hockey trivia. The fact was the Penguins, just ten months after winning the Stanley Cup, had faltered in the post-season's second round. "It's definitely disappointing," Crosby said after the game. "Game seven, anything can happen and, unfortunately, we weren't at our best."

Beyond the loss to Montreal, Crosby did receive small post-season consolation when he was announced as a finalist for the Hart Trophy as the NHL's most valuable player. He had won it before in 2006–07, and this time he was up against rival Alexander Ovechkin and Vancouver Canucks forward Henrik Sedin. Crosby would be disappointed again, as Henrik Sedin won the award with forty-six first-place ballots. Ovechkin finished second with forty, and Crosby came in third with twenty first-place votes.

IS THE BEST YET TO COME?

Heading into the 2009–10 regular season, Sidney Crosby's main goal was to hoist the Stanley Cup once again. So by that measure the year must be viewed as a disappointment. But a glance at the previous twelve months proved that Crosby had experienced incredible success: a Stanley Cup championship followed by a memorable parade and celebration in his home province of Nova Scotia; Olympic hockey team selection followed by scoring the gold medal winning goal on home ice; and a share of the Maurice "Rocket" Richard Trophy as the NHL's co-leading scorer with 51 goals.

Not bad for a year that ended in so-called disappointment. But the disappointment has to be considered temporary. In a life already crammed with the achievement of excellence, Crosby had amassed a breathtaking quantity of success in a short time. The Stanley Cup victory proved that he, like Wayne Gretzky and Mario Lemieux, was a winner who had the ability to lead his team to a championship at a young age. And his game-winning goal against the Americans elevated his star status to truly Olympian heights. Before the goal he was a superstar, a brand-name professional athlete who was the leading man of the National Hockey League, a player whose image was part of several high-profile corporate endorsements, like Reebok, Tim Horton's, and Gatorade. After the goal, he was a cultural icon. He brought a smile to an entire nation. Even people who didn't like him—Crosby haters—cheered lustily when he beat Ryan Miller to score the winning goal in Vancouver.

Many years ago, Sidney Crosby said, "I want to be the best. So whatever comes with that, I have to accept it." If he only knew then what we know now. Sidney Crosby has already proven he's the best—or at least one of a chosen few. What has come with that mantle are incredible expectations. From now on, when he scores, wins major awards, or hoists championship trophies, he's merely accomplishing what the hockey world has grown to expect from him. When he fails—like he and his team did in the second round of the 2010 Stanley Cup playoffs, the scrutiny and criticism becomes intense, perhaps not commensurate with the situation. But we should be reminded that this is what Crosby himself wanted.

He has accepted it. He is not a king, nor does he wear a crown, but Sidney Crosby does hold a high station in the NHL. He's the star of his generation, the one everyone wants to watch, meet, and interview—and Crosby does not carry the burden of celebrity like it's an unbearable burden. Rather, he does it with elegance, dignity, and above all else, respect. A product of a terrific family, a celebrated member of a proud community, and the recipient of some incredible hockey genes, Sidney Crosby is arguably the most famous and most accomplished hockey player in the world, and he's only twenty-three years old.

Statistics

MAJOR AWARDS

QMJHL	
RDS/JVC Trophy (rookie of the year)	2004
Michel Brière Memorial Trophy (most valuable player)	2004, 2005
Jean Béliveau Trophy (league leading scorer)	2004, 2005
Mike Bossy Trophy (best professional prospect)	2005
Paul Dumont Trophy (personality of the year)	2004, 2005
Guy Lafleur Trophy (playoff MVP)	2005
Michel Bergeron Trophy (offensive rookie of the year)	2004
Offensive Player of the Year	2004, 2005

CHL	
CHL Rookie of the Year	2004
CHL Player of the Year	2004, 2005
Leading Scorer	2004, 2005
Top Pro Prospect	2005
Ed Chynoweth Trophy (Memorial Cup leading scorer)	2005

NHL	
Art Ross Trophy (leading scorer)	2007
Lester B. Pearson Award (best player as voted by peers)	2007
Hart Memorial Trophy (most valuable player in the NHL)	2007
Rocket Richard Trophy (goals leader)	2010

Other	
Lou Marsh Trophy	2007, 2009
Lionel Conacher Award	2007, 2009
The Order of Nova Scotia	2008

NHL

Season	Team	League	REGULAR SEASON					PLAYOFFS				
			GP	G	A	Pts	PIM	GP	G	A	Pts	PIM
1999–00	Cole Harbour Red Wings	Peewee AAA	~70	—	—	~200	—	—	—	—	—	—
1999–00	Cole Harbour Red Wings	Bantam AAA	1	1	3	4	—	—	—	—	—	—
2000–01	Cole Harbour Red Wings	Bantam AAA	63	86	96	182	—	5	10	6	16	—
2001–02	Dartmouth Subways	Midget AAA	74	95	98	193	114	7	11	13	24	0
2002–03	Shattuck St. Mary's	USHS	57	72	90	162	104	—	—	—	—	—
2003–04	Rimouski Océanic	QMJHL	59	54	81	135	74	9	7	9	16	10
2004–05	Rimouski Océanic	QMJHL	62	66	102	168	84	13	14	17	31	16
2005–06	Pittsburgh Penguins	NHL	81	39	63	102	110	—	—	—	—	—
2006–07	Pittsburgh Penguins	NHL	79	36	84	120	60	5	3	2	5	4
2007–08	Pittsburgh Penguins	NHL	53	24	48	72	39	20	6	21	27	12
2008–09	Pittsburgh Penguins	NHL	77	33	70	103	76	24	15	16	31	14
2009–10	Pittsburgh Penguins	NHL	81	51	58	109	69	13	6	13	19	6
NHL totals	371	183	323	506	354	62	30	52	82	36		

International competition

Year	Team	Comp	GP	G	A	Pts	PIM
2003	Canada	JWC18	5	4	2	6	10
2004	Canada	WJC	6	2	3	5	4
2005	Canada	WJC	6	6	3	9	4
2006	Canada	WC	9	8	8	16	10
2010	Canada	OLY	7	4	3	7	4

Statistics and award data from: hockeydb.com, tsn.ca, espn.com, nhl.com, hockeycanada.ca

Image Credits

About the Author

Paul Hollingsworth is CTV Atlantic's recognized sports authority and the Atlantic correspondent for TSN. As a result of his passionate and knowledgeable sports coverage, he won a Gemini Award in 2003. Paul is the author of *Brad Richards*, and co-author of *All Sorts of Sports Trivia*. He lives in Dartmouth, Nova Scotia.